"Through an introductory study of John Calvin's preaching, Steve Lawson provides a practical Homiletics I refresher course that can be read in one evening, but should be read annually for lifelong impact. Factual yet stimulating, simple yet penetrating, *The Expository Genius of John Calvin* contains many scriptural and theocentric golden nuggets and hands-on practical tips for beginning expositors and seasoned preachers alike. May God use it to revitalize Christ-centered and Spirit-empowered applicatory preaching in our needy day."

— Dr. Joel R. Beeke, Professor
Puritan Reformed Theological Seminary

"An infectious appreciation of the preaching of John Calvin from the pen of Steven Lawson. No one reading this volume can fail to appreciate the debt we owe to the 'Genevan Reformer.' Lawson has consulted the best of current scholarship and has produced a comprehensive distillation of the contours of the Reformer's preaching and, with it, a compelling advocacy of consecutive expository preaching. A magnificent achievement."

— Dr. Derek W. H. Thomas, Professor
Reformed Theological Seminary

"Calvin's commitment to 'the word of God,' whether as inscripturated or incarnate in Christ, is well-known. What has not been given its due, however, is his high regard for 'words'— both the words of the Old and New Testament in their original languages and of the preacher in his sermons on the sacred text. Steve Lawson's study treats the second closely, and this is where this book will prove most valuable and is most urgently needed."

— Dr. Hywel R. Jones, Professor
Westminster Seminary California

"The cure for the 'dys-exposition' that afflicts today's pulpits has been available for five hundred years, as Steve Lawson so clearly documents in *The Expository Genius of John Calvin*. Preachers reading this book will be moved to take to heart Calvin's encompassing belief in the sovereignty of God's Word—as to its total sufficiency and massive potency. Further, they will be inspired to pursue the deep, enriching paths of *lectio continua*. This is a beautifully written, powerful, and convincing book. It is a must read for all who aspire to preach the word."

— R. KENT HUGHES, Senior pastor emeritus
College Church, Wheaton, Ill.

"In this book, Dr. Steve Lawson has masterfully presented us with thirty-two keynotes that made Calvin the best preacher of the Reformation, all of them centered around the Word of God preached expositorily. He describes for us in a powerful as well as profound way how Calvin brought his congregation upward to gaze upon God's glory as he preached verse by verse, then ended his sermons with prayers filled with the Word! Dr. Lawson is right in saying that because of the spiritual bankruptcy of our time, we need Calvins once again. I would make this book recommended reading in courses such as homiletics and missions for any serious pastor and student of theology."

— DR. ALONZO RAMÍREZ, Professor
Biblical Reformed Seminary, Peru

THE EXPOSITORY GENIUS
of JOHN CALVIN

A **Long Line of Godly Men** Profile

The Expository Genius *of*

John Calvin

STEVEN J. LAWSON

℞

Reformation Trust

PUBLISHING

A DIVISION OF LIGONIER MINISTRIES · ORLANDO, FLORIDA

The Expository Genius of John Calvin
© 2007 by Steven J. Lawson

Published by Reformation Trust
a division of Ligonier Ministries
400 Technology Park, Lake Mary, FL 32746

Printed in the United States of America

Cover design: Chris Larson
Cover illustration: Kent Barton
Interior design and typeset: Katherine Lloyd, Sisters, Ore.

Unless otherwise indicated, all Scripture quotations are from The Holy Bible, English Standard Version, copyright © 2001 by Crossway Bibles, a division of Good News Publishers. Used by permission. All rights reserved.

Library of Congress Cataloging-in-Publication Data

Lawson, Steven J.
 The expository genius of John Calvin / by Steven J. Lawson.
    p. cm. -- (The "long line of godly men" profile series)
 Includes bibliographical references.
 ISBN 1-56769-085-8 (978-1-56769-085-9)
 1. Calvin, Jean, 1509-1564. 2. Preaching--History--16th century. I. Title.
 BX9418.L37 2006
 251.0092--dc22
                                                    2006039064

To John MacArthur—
faithful shepherd, peerless expositor,
defender of the faith.

For almost forty years, Dr. MacArthur has stood in the pulpit at Grace Community Church and has been the gold standard of biblical exposition for an entire generation of preachers. His masterful preaching through books of the Bible, as well as his New Testament commentaries, study Bible, seminary, college, missionary academy, and worldwide radio ministry, make him, I believe, the John Calvin of our day.

For we do not preach ourselves but Christ Jesus as Lord,
and ourselves as your bond-servants for Jesus' sake.
(2 COR. 4:5, NASB)

Contents

Standing on Holy Ground

To step into the pulpit is to enter onto holy ground. To stand behind an open Bible demands no trifling with sacred things. To be a spokesman for God requires utmost concern and care in handling and proclaiming the Word. Rightly does Scripture warn, "Not many of you should become teachers, my brothers, for you know that we who teach will be judged with greater strictness" (James 3:1).

But sad to say, we live in a generation that has compromised this sacred calling to preach. Exposition is being replaced with entertainment, preaching with performances, doctrine with drama, and theology with theatrics. Desperately does the modern-day church need to recover its way and return to a pulpit that is Bible-based, Christ-centered, and life-changing. God has always been pleased to honor His Word—especially His Word *preached*. The greatest seasons of church history—those eras of widespread reformation and great awakening—have been those epochs in which God-fearing men took the inspired Word and unashamedly preached it in the power of the Holy Spirit. As the pulpit goes, so goes the church. Thus, only a reformed pulpit will ultimately lead to a reformed church. In this hour, pastors must see their pulpits again marked by sequential exposition, doctrinal clarity, and a sense of gravity regarding eternal matters. This, in my estimation, is *the* need of the hour.

This book is the first of a series that will examine the varied ministries of noted men from church history. Given the pressing need in our time for powerful pulpits, preachers will be a key focus. The reason for this emphasis is simple—I can think of no better discipline for preachers today, apart from the study of Scripture itself, than to examine the biblical exposition of spiritual giants from the past.

To that end, this book will investigate the preaching of the great Reformer of Geneva, John Calvin. Future books in this series will delve into the ministries of other gifted preachers, such as Martin Luther, George Whitefield, Jonathan Edwards, Charles Spurgeon, and others. These mighty men were used by God to reform the church, confront the world, and alter the flow of history. At the very epicenters of these extraordinary ministries were pulpits that were anchored to the Word. In a very real sense, these pulpits were the hinges upon which history turned.

As we look back upon those men and the momentous

times in which they lived, certain questions must be raised: What marked the preaching of these influential men? What were their commitments in the public proclamation of the Word? The approaches these men took to the pulpit must receive our closest attention if we are to see another great movement of God in our day.

As we consider Calvin's life and work, we will survey the distinguishing marks of his pulpit ministry, consider the core presuppositions that undergirded his biblical preaching, and examine his personal preparation for the pulpit. Along the way, we will gain an overview of his preaching itself—his sermon introduction, interpretation, application, conclusion, and final intercession. In short, we will explore the distinguishing marks of Calvin's expository genius.

The goal here is not to take a sentimental journey—the hour is too desperate for such a triviality. Rather, the aim of this book is to raise the bar for a new generation of expositors. The method is to see what a commitment to biblical preaching looks like by examining the work of a man who was sold out to this sacred duty.

If you are a preacher or teacher, may you be challenged to a higher standard in your handling of the Word. If you are a supporter of one called to this ministry, may you know how best to pray. May all who read these chapters find them impactful and inspirational, mighty and motivational—all for the ushering in of a new reformation.

I want to express my gratitude to the team at Ligonier

Ministries for their keen interest and involvement in this project. Tim Dick, president and chief executive of Ligonier, first saw the value in this book being placed in your hands. Greg Bailey, director of publications for Ligonier's Reformation Trust Publishing division, did a masterful job of fine-tuning my work, and Creative Director Chris Larson added his talented touch to the graphic design.

At Christ Fellowship Baptist Church, I want to thank the elders, pastors, and congregation, who urged me to pursue God's will in writing this book. I also want to thank my executive assistant, Kay Allen, who typed this document and coordinated the efforts, and Keith Phillips and Mark Hassler, who provided invaluable help in researching and working with the manuscript.

At home, my wife, Anne, and our four children, Andrew, James, Grace Anne, and John, have only encouraged me in my writing assignments. May all who read this book know the loving home environment in which I study and write.

Soli Deo Gloria.

—Steven J. Lawson
Mobile, Alabama
September 2006

CHAPTER ONE

Calvin's Life
and Legacy

*Calvin had no weapon but the Bible. . . . Calvin
preached from the Bible every day, and under the
power of that preaching the city began to be trans-
formed. As the people of Geneva acquired knowledge
of God's Word and were changed by it, the city
became, as John Knox called it later, a New Jerusalem
from which the gospel spread to the rest of Europe,
England, and the New World.*[1]

—JAMES MONTGOMERY BOICE

Towering over the centuries of church history, there stands
one figure of such monumental importance that he still
commands attention and arouses intrigue, even five hundred
years after his appearance on the world stage. Called "one of
the truly great men of all time,"[2] he was a driving force so
significant that his influence shaped the church and Western

1

culture beyond that of any other theologian or pastor. His masterful expositions of Scripture laid down the doctrinal distinctives of the Protestant Reformation, making him arguably the leading architect of the Protestant cause. His theological thunder defined and articulated the core truths of that history-altering movement in sixteenth-century Europe. In turn, those lofty ideas helped fashion the founding principles of Western civilization, giving rise to the republican form of government, the ideals of public education, and the philosophy of free-market capitalism.[3] A world-class theologian, a revered exegete, a renowned teacher, an ecclesiastical statesman, an influential Reformer—he was all of these and more. His name was John Calvin.

First and foremost, however, Calvin was a *pastor*—the faithful shepherd for twenty-five years to a local flock in Geneva, Switzerland. Every pastor has many demands on his time, and Calvin, because of his status in Geneva, had more responsibilities than most. Reformation historian J. H. Merle D'Aubigné wrote:

On Sundays [Calvin] conducted divine service, and had daily service every other week. He devoted three hours in each week to theological teaching; he visited the sick, and administered private reproof. He received strangers; attended the consistory on Thursday, and directed its deliberations; on Friday was present at the conference on Scripture, called the *congregation*; and, after the minister in office for the day had presented his views on some passage of Scripture, and the other pastors had made their remarks, Calvin added some observations, which were *a kind of lecture*. . . . The week in which he did not preach was filled up with other duties; and he had duties of every kind. In particular, he devoted much attention to the refugees who flocked to Geneva, driven by persecution out of France and Italy; he taught and exhorted them. He consoled, by his letters, "those who were still in the jaws of the lion"; he interceded for them. In his study he threw light on the sacred writings by admirable commentaries, and confuted the writings of the enemies of the gospel.[4]

But amid these many pastoral duties, Calvin was primarily a *preacher*, a biblical expositor of the highest order. Indeed, the German Reformer Philip Melanchthon labeled him simply "the theologian," an indication of the respect Calvin was accorded for his abilities as an interpreter of Scripture. In his years in Geneva, Calvin viewed the pulpit as his principal responsibility, the first work of his pastoral calling. Thus, this magisterial Reformer gave himself to the exposition of the Word as perhaps no one else in history. He esteemed and elevated biblical preaching to be of highest importance, and so he made it his lifelong commitment.

As a result, apart from the biblical authors themselves, Calvin stands today as the most influential minister of the

Word of God the world has ever seen. No man before or since has been so prolific and so penetrating in his handling of Scripture. Calvin's exegetical insights address most of the Old Testament and all of the New Testament except Revelation. By overwhelming consent, he remains the greatest biblical commentator of all time. On his deathbed, when Calvin reviewed his many accomplishments, he mentioned his sermons ahead of even his vast writings. For Calvin, preaching was job number one.

THE REAL CALVIN

This estimation of the priority of biblical preaching in Calvin's ministry is not novel. No less an authority than Emile Doumergue, the foremost biographer of Calvin, stood in the great Reformer's pulpit in 1909 to mark the four-hundredth anniversary of Calvin's birth, and said: "That is the Calvin who seems to me to be the real and authentic Calvin, the one who explains all the others: Calvin the preacher of Geneva, moulding by his words the spirit of the Reformed of the sixteenth century."[5] In that same memorable address, Doumergue remarked: "While he has come to be remembered as a theologian who recovered the doctrinal landmarks which had been buried under the debris of confused centuries, or as a powerful controversialist whose name opponents have sought to fasten upon beliefs which they judged odious, the truth is that Calvin saw himself, first of all, as a pastor in the church of Christ and therefore as one whose chief duty must be to preach the Word."[6]

D'Aubigné has likewise affirmed the primacy of Calvin's preaching amid his many ministries. Calvin's principal office, D'Aubigné remarked, was the one he assigned to the minister: to proclaim the Word of God for instruction, admonition, exhortation, and reproof. To this end, Calvin's preaching was replete with practical instruction and application, which he saw as a fundamental necessity.[7] Thus, according to D'Aubigné, Calvin's chief mission was the explication and application of the Holy Scriptures. This was the *real* Calvin—the biblical expositor who considered the pulpit to be "the heart of his ministry."[8]

If the real Calvin was preeminently a preacher, who was Calvin the *man*? What was the road God marked out for him to travel? What were the times in which he lived? What were his accomplishments? More important, what contributed to his greatness? We will address these questions and more in this chapter before turning our attention to Calvin's expository genius.

CALVIN THE MAN

The world into which Calvin was born was ripe for reformation. At Calvin's birth, Martin Luther was 26 years old and already had commenced his teaching ministry at the University of Wittenberg. Eight years later, in 1517, the German Reformer posted his Ninety-Five Theses on the door of the Castle Church at Wittenberg, a protest that proved to be "the shot heard round the world." The Diet of Worms followed (1521), where Luther took his now-famous stand for the Word of God. Soon after, Reformation fires began to burn brightly in Germany and to spread rapidly across Europe into Scotland and England, especially to the universities. Meanwhile, the five *solas* of the Reformation—salvation by *grace alone*, through *faith alone*, in *Christ alone*, to the *glory of God alone*, based on *Scripture alone*—were being forged on the anvils of minds that were being renewed in the Scriptures.

John Calvin—his French name was Jean Cauvin—was born to Gerard and Jeanne Cauvin on July 10, 1509, in the farm country of Noyon, France, sixty miles northeast of Paris. Calvin's father, a financial administrator for the Catholic bishop of the Noyon diocese, raised his son to enter the priesthood in the Roman Catholic Church. When John was 11, Gerard used his influence to gain a chaplaincy for his son at the Noyon Cathedral. Then, when John was 14, he entered the University of Paris to study theology in formal preparation to become a priest. Calvin's time at the university resulted in a master of arts degree at age 17. But more important, this future Reformer emerged with a solid grounding in the basics of a classical education, including Latin, logic, and philosophy.

Upon Calvin's graduation from the University of Paris, his father attempted to gain two more appointments for him in the Catholic Church. But a conflict with the bishop of Noyon prompted Gerard to redirect his brilliant son to study law at the University of Orléans (1528). During his time there, and later at the University of Bourges, Calvin learned Greek, the powers of analytical thinking, and persuasive argument, skills later to be used in his Genevan pulpit. Armed with such abilities, Calvin would later be nicknamed "the accusative case" for his penchant to argue his point convincingly.

When Gerard died (1531), the 21-year-old Calvin was freed from his father's dominant influence and moved back to Paris to pursue his first love, the study of literature, especially the classics. He later returned to Bourges, where he completed his legal studies and received his doctor of laws degree (1532). In that same year, Calvin published his first book, a secular treatment of *De Clementia* (*On Mercy*) by the Roman philosopher Seneca the Younger. The book, which was Calvin's doctoral dissertation, revealed his growing ability to break down language and grasp the intentions of an author. In the future, this was precisely what Calvin would do with the Scriptures, both in the pulpit and in print—giving the God-intended meaning by explaining the message of the biblical writers.

A SUDDEN CONVERSION

It was while he was studying at Bourges that Calvin came in direct contact with the biblical truths of the Reformation. Upon being introduced to the gospel, a growing restlessness with his way of life came upon him, and a deepening conviction of his sin drove him to seek relief in the grace and mercy of God. Here is how Calvin later described his encounter with Christ and its immediate effects:

> God by a sudden conversion subdued and brought my mind to a teachable frame, which was more hardened in such matters than might have been expected from one at my early period of life. Having thus received some taste and knowledge of true godliness, I was immediately inflamed with so intense a desire to make progress therein, that although I did not altogether leave off other studies, yet I pursued them with less ardour.[9]

Of this "sudden conversion," Alexandre Ganoczy wrote, "Calvin understood his life story as analogous to that of the Apostle Paul, who on the way to Damascus, suddenly turned from the sin of opposing Christ to unconditionally serving Christ."[10] Indeed, Calvin emulated Paul in that, upon his conversion, he immediately changed his allegiance, abandoning the Roman Catholic Church to join the growing Protestant cause.

REFORMER IN THE MAKING

Calvin soon met opposition for his new faith in Christ. In November 1533, Nicolas Cop, rector of the University of Paris and a friend of Calvin, preached the opening address of the winter term at the university, which was "a plea for a reformation on the basis of the New Testament, and a bold attack on the scholastic theologians of the day."[11] However, Cop encountered strong resistance for his expressed "Luther-like" views. Calvin, who is believed to have written the speech for Cop, was forced to flee Paris in the middle of the night, lowering himself out a window by means of sheets and escaping to safety in the guise of a vinedresser with a hoe on his shoulder. This virulent opposition was but a harbinger of things to come for the rest of Calvin's life.

After suffering imprisonment for a short time, Calvin fled to the estate of Louis du Tillet, a well-to-do man who was sympathetic to the Reformation cause. In this "quiet nest," as Calvin described it, he had the opportunity to spend five months in du Tillet's extensive theological library. There he read the Bible, along with the writings of the church fathers, most notably Augustine. By hard work, genius, and grace, Calvin was becoming a self-taught theologian of no small stature.

Finally, under the deepening conviction of the truth of Scripture, Calvin renounced the income he had been drawing from the Catholic Church since childhood for his supposed Noyon pastorate. The die was cast. He was fully aligned with the truths and cause of the Reformation.

After a brief journey to Paris and Orléans, Calvin went to Basel, Switzerland (1534–1536), and began writing his magnum opus, *Institutes of the Christian Religion*. Calvin's *Institutes* would become the defining masterpiece of Protestant theology, the single most important book to be written during the Reformation. It would take its place ahead of even Luther's most revered work, *The Bondage of the Will.* During the next twenty-three years, the *Institutes* would undergo five major expansions until reaching its present form in 1559. Addressed to King Francis I of France, this work explained the true nature of biblical Christianity. Calvin hoped the book would ease the persecution that was being brought against Protestants by the Roman Catholic Church in France. It was a theological tour de force, presenting a compelling argument for core Reformed teachings, and its publication instantly thrust Calvin into a recognized leadership role among the Reformers.

To Geneva: A Strange Providence

When a temporary amnesty was granted to French exiles, Calvin quickly returned to France, where he gathered his brother, Antoine, and sister, Marie. He then set out for Strasbourg, then in southern Germany, intending to study and write in seclusion and tranquility. He would never return to his homeland.

While en route to Strasbourg, however, Calvin was providentially redirected. A war between Charles V, the Holy Roman emperor, and Francis I resulted in troop movements that blocked the road to Strasbourg, and Calvin was forced to detour through Geneva, Switzerland, nestled under the snow-capped Alps on the shores of Lake Geneva, the largest lake in Europe. Calvin intended to spend only one night there, but he was recognized by William Farel, the Protestant leader in this newly Reformed city. Their meeting proved to be one of history's most pivotal encounters, not just for the church in Geneva, but for the world. As Calvin later recounted it:

> Farel, who burned with an extraordinary zeal to advance the gospel, immediately strained every nerve to detain me. And after having learned that my heart was set upon devoting myself to private studies, for which I wished to keep myself free from other pursuits, and finding that he gained nothing by entreaties, he proceeded to utter an imprecation that God would curse my retirement, and the tranquility of the studies which I sought, if I should withdraw and refuse to give assistance, when the necessity was so urgent. By this imprecation I was so stricken with terror, that I desisted from the journey which I had undertaken.[12]

In response to Farel's challenge—"If you do not assist us in this work of the Lord, the Lord will punish you"[13]—the young theologian agreed to stay, acknowledging that this was the direction of God for his life. Rather than study in the cloistered quietness of Strasbourg, Calvin was suddenly thrust into the visible spotlight of Geneva, with its many demands. He was first appointed professor of sacred Scripture in Geneva, then, four months later, pastor of Saint Pierre Cathedral.

BANISHED TO STRASBOURG

Calvin and Farel immediately began working to reform the church in Geneva. Drawing up a confession of faith and oath, they audaciously sought to bring the lives of the ten thousand citizens of the city into conformity with Scripture. But they soon met strong opposition. Their attempts to fence the Lord's Table by excommunication—that is, restricting those living in open sin from partaking of the elements—resulted in their banishment from the city in 1538.

Once again, Calvin went into exile, this time to Strasbourg, the place he had intended to go to study and write. For three years (1538–1541), Calvin pastored a Protestant congregation of some five hundred French-speaking refugees in Strasbourg. He also taught the New Testament in the local theological institute, wrote his first commentary (on Romans), and published the second edition of the *Institutes*.

During these years in Strasbourg, Calvin also found a wife, Idelette Stordeur, a member of his congregation. An Anabaptist widow, she had a son and a daughter from her first marriage.[14] They married in 1540, when Calvin was 31. In future years, this union would bring much heartache to his soul. Idelette would miscarry once, lose a daughter at birth, and deliver a son who would die at two weeks of age. Calvin later wrote, "The Lord has certainly inflicted a bitter wound in the death of our infant son. But He is Himself a father and knows what is good for His children."[15] Idelette herself would die of tuberculosis in 1549 at age 40. Calvin would never remarry. For the rest of his life, he would devote himself to the work of the Lord with singular vision.

RETURNING TO GENEVA

Meanwhile, the City Council of Geneva found itself in much struggle, and called for Calvin to return as the city's pastor. After a ten-month hesitation, he reluctantly accepted the invitation, knowing that much hostility awaited. Calvin re-entered the city on September 13, 1541, never to relocate again. In Geneva, he made his mark as the Reformed church leader and the Reformation's brightest light.

Upon his return, Calvin hit the town preaching. Reassuming his pulpit ministry precisely where he had left off three years earlier—in the very *next* verse of his earlier exposition—Calvin became a mainstay, preaching multiple times on Sunday and, during some weeks, each weekday. His verse-by-verse exposition of Scripture, week after week, even day after day, would make Geneva a shining beacon of truth.

During this tumultuous time, French Protestants, known as Huguenots; Protestant saints from Scotland and England, who were escaping the martyr's stake of "Bloody Mary"; and refugees from Germany and Italy began pouring into Geneva, seeking safety from the life-threatening dangers they faced in their native lands. In a short time, Geneva's population doubled to more than twenty thousand. The city was alive with students of the Word, and Calvin was their teacher.

Among these refugees from abroad was a Scotsman named John Knox, who commended Calvin's church in Geneva as "the most perfect school of Christ that ever was in the earth since the days of the Apostles."[16] While in Geneva, Knox was part of a team of Protestant exiles who sat under Calvin's exposition and translated the Geneva Bible for English-speaking refugees. It was the first Bible to have theological notes printed in the margin, a direct extension of Calvin's pulpit. This Bible became the predominant Bible among English Puritans for the next one hundred years. Additionally, it became the official version of the Scottish Protestant church and the household Bible of English-speaking Protestants everywhere. The Pilgrims brought the Geneva Bible with them on the Mayflower to America, and it became the Bible of choice among the early Colonists.

AN EXPANDING INFLUENCE

As the chief expositor of Scripture in a bastion of biblical teaching, Calvin found himself wielding an international influence of no small proportions. A thousand of the men who had fled to Geneva to sit under his preaching eventually returned to France, carrying biblical truth with them. Knox later became the leader of the Reformation in Scotland. Others left Calvin's side to plant Reformed churches in anti-Protestant countries such as Hungary, Holland, and England. Because persecution was certain and martyrdom common for these saints, Calvin's school of theology became known as "Calvin's School of Death."

The printing press also spread Calvin's influence. During this time, a man named Denis Raguenier began taking down Calvin's sermons for his own use by means of a private system of shorthand. Eventually, he was employed to produce a transcript of each one-hour sermon, which contained about six thousand words. Raguenier did his work with amazing accuracy, hardly a word escaping him. These written expositions were soon translated into various languages, gaining a far-reaching distribution. Scotland and England especially came under the sway of Calvin's pulpit via the printed page. Later, the Synod of Dort in Holland (1618–1619) and the Westminster Assembly in England (1643–1649), which drafted the Westminster Confession and Catechisms, became indirect outgrowths of Calvin's biblical preaching. To this day, many of Calvin's sermons remain in print.

IN THE FACE OF ADVERSITY

For Calvin, these prolific years in Geneva were anything but an "ivory tower" experience. While ascending his pulpit regularly, he met much difficulty on every side. Frail in stature, Calvin suffered many ailments. He also endured physical threats to his life. Yet Calvin never ceased his exposition.

Further, groups of Geneva's citizens caused him much pain, not the least of them being the Libertines, who boasted in sinful licentiousness. Sexual immorality was permissible, they claimed, arguing that the "communion of the saints" meant that their bodies should be joined to the wives of others. The Libertines openly practiced adultery and yet desired to come to the Lord's Table. But Calvin would have none of it.

In an epic encounter, Philibert Berthelier, a prominent Libertine, was excommunicated because of his known sexual promiscuity. Consequently, he was forbidden from partaking of the Lord's Supper. Through the underhanded influence of the Libertines, the City Council overrode the church's decision, and Berthelier and his associates came to church to take the Lord's Supper with swords drawn, ready to fight. With bold audacity, Calvin descended from the pulpit, stood in front of the Communion table, and said, "These hands you may crush, these arms you may lop off, my life you may take, my blood is yours, you may shed it; but you shall never force me to give holy things to the profaned and dishonor the table of my God."[17] Berthelier and the Libertines withdrew, no match for such unflinching convictions.

FAITHFUL TO THE END

As the end of his life approached, Calvin faced death as he had faced the pulpit—with great resolution. The theocentricity of his faith appears in his last will and testament, which he dictated on April 25, 1564:

> In the name of God, I, John Calvin, servant of the Word of God in the church of Geneva, . . . thank God that He has shown not only mercy toward me, His poor creature, and . . . has suffered me in all sins and weaknesses, but what is much more, that He has made me a partaker of His grace to serve Him through my work. . . . I confess to live and die in this faith which He has given me, inasmuch as I have no other hope or refuge than His predestination upon which my entire salvation is grounded. I embrace the grace which He has offered me in our Lord Jesus Christ and accept the merits of His suffering and dying, that through them all my sins are buried; and I humbly beg Him to wash me and cleanse me with the blood of our great Redeemer, . . . so that I, when I shall appear before His face may bear His likeness. Moreover, I declare that I endeavored to teach His Word undefiled and to expound Holy Scripture faithfully, according to the measure of grace which He has given me.[18]

Calvin died at age 54 on May 27, 1564, in the arms of Theodore Beza, his successor. Looking back on Calvin's life, Beza concluded:

Having been a spectator of his conduct for sixteen years, I have given a faithful account both of his life and of his death, and I can now declare, that in him all men may see a most beautiful example of Christian Character, an example which it is as easy to slander as it is difficult to imitate.[19]

It is appropriate that Calvin's last words—"How long, O Lord?"—were the words of Scripture. He literally died quoting the Bible he preached, having expended himself in the work and will of God, faithful to the very end.

CALVIN: A PREACHER FOR THE AGES

Given the momentous life of the Genevan Reformer, and especially his devotion to the pulpit, certain questions beg to be asked: What kind of preacher was this remarkable man? How did he approach this sacred duty of expositing the Word of God? What were the distinctive features of his famed pulpit? And what can present-day preachers learn from him? What follows in this book is an attempt to set forth the distinguishing marks of Calvin's expository genius.

As a result of this study, my prayer is that now more than ever, those who stand behind the sacred desk would recover the vanishing art of expository preaching. The church is always looking for better *methods* in order to reach the world. But God is looking for better *men* who will devote themselves to

His biblically mandated method for advancing His kingdom, namely, preaching—and not just any kind of preaching, but *expository* preaching.

This being so, nothing could be more relevant for preachers in this hour—a time when fads and gimmicks seem to be hypnotizing church leaders—than to revisit the pulpit power of the Genevan Reformer. May a new generation of expositors arise to embrace his core distinctives in their preaching ministries.

Notes

1. James Montgomery Boice, *Whatever Happened to the Gospel of Grace? Rediscovering the Doctrines that Shook the World* (Wheaton, IL: Crossway Books, 2001), 83–84.
2. Curt Daniel, *The History and Theology of Calvinism* (Dallas, TX: Scholarly Reprints, 1993), 24.
3. For further reading, see Alister E. McGrath, *A Life of John Calvin: A Study in the Shaping of Western Culture* (Oxford, England, and Malden, MA: Blackwell Publishing, 1990, 2001), 219–261; John T. McNeill, *The History and Character of Calvinism* (London, England; Oxford, England; and New York, NY: Oxford University Press, 1954, 1967), 411–425; and Jeannine E. Olson, "Calvin and Social-Ethical Issues," in *The Cambridge Companion to John Calvin*, ed. Donald K. McKim (Cambridge, England: Cambridge University Press, 2004), 153–172.
4. J. H. Merle D'Aubigné, *History of the Reformation in Europe in the Time of Calvin, Vol. VII* (Harrisonburg, VA: Sprinkle Publications, 1880, 2000), 82.
5. Publisher's introduction, "John Calvin and His Sermons on Ephesians," in John Calvin, *Sermons on the Epistle to the Ephesians* (Carlisle, PA, and Edinburgh, Scotland: The Banner of Truth Trust, 1562, 1577, 1973, 1975, 1979, 1987, 1998), viii.
6. Ibid.
7. D'Aubigné, *History of the Reformation in Europe in the Time of Calvin, Vol. VII*, 82.

8. Douglas Kelly, introduction to John Calvin, *Sermons on 2 Samuel: Chapters 1–13*, trans. Douglas Kelly (Carlisle, PA, and Edinburgh, Scotland: The Banner of Truth Trust, 1992), ix.

9. Calvin, preface to *Commentary on the Book of Psalms*, trans. James Anderson (Edinburgh, Scotland: Calvin Translation Society, 1845; reprinted by Baker Books, 2003), xl–xli.

10. Alexandre Ganoczy, "Calvin's life," trans. David L. Foxgrover and James Schmitt, in *The Cambridge Companion to John Calvin*, 9.

11. Philip Schaff, *History of the Christian Church, Vol. VIII* (Grand Rapids, MI: Eerdmans Publishing Co., 1910, 1984), 318.

12. Calvin, preface to *Commentary on the Book of Psalms*, xlii–xliii.

13. Theodore Beza, *The Life of John Calvin,* trans. Henry Beveridge (Edinburgh, Scotland: Calvin Translation Society, 1844; reprinted by Back Home Industries, 1996), 26.

14. William J. Bouwsma, *John Calvin: A Sixteenth-Century Portrait* (New York, NY, and Oxford, England: Oxford University Press, 1988), 23.

15. Beza, *The Life of John Calvin*, 134.

16. Schaff, *History of the Christian Church, Vol. VIII*, 518.

17. William Wileman, *John Calvin: His Life, His Teaching, and His Influence* (Choteau, MT: Old Paths Gospel Press), 96. This famous line has also been rendered as: "I will die sooner than this hand shall stretch forth the sacred things of the Lord to those who have been judged despisers." Beza, *The Life of John Calvin*, 71.

18. Beza, *The Life of John Calvin*, 99–103.

19. Ibid., 117.

CHAPTER TWO

Approaching the Pulpit

Calvin was no Genevan dictator, ruling the population with a rod of iron. He was not even a citizen of Geneva throughout his time there, and was thus denied access to political authority. His status was simply that of a pastor who was in no position to dictate to the magisterial authorities who administered the city. . . . Calvin's influence over Geneva rested ultimately not in his formal legal standing (which was insignificant) but in his considerable personal authority as a preacher and pastor.[1]

—ALISTER E. MCGRATH

As the sun rises on another Lord's Day morning in mid-sixteenth-century Geneva, the majestic edifice of Saint Pierre Cathedral can be seen soaring high above the rooftops of the city. Inside, the vaulted ceiling rises to an enormous height far above the entire length of the sanctuary. A soul-gripping awe and a mind-stretching transcendence fill the worshipers who enter this sanctuary. But the grandeur of God is most clearly displayed here through the preaching of the infallible Word. This former Roman Catholic bastion is now a fortress of biblical truth. It has become a house of Reformed worship—a place where the exposition of Scripture is preeminent.

Citizens of Geneva gather here, increasingly imbibing the doctrinal truths of the Protestant Reformation. Along with them come beleaguered French Huguenots who have fled the tyranny of their Rome-entrenched homeland. Refugees also gather from Scotland and England, having escaped martyrdom at the hands of "Bloody Mary." And other exiles pour in from throughout Europe, including Germany and Italy.

For one small group of French Huguenots, newly arrived in Geneva, this is a momentous occasion. Their previous worship experience was an isolated gathering with a few fellow believers, huddled behind a barn in France. Hunted like prey, they hid from the royal dragoon guards of the king of France. Having eluded these specially trained and armed soldiers at the border, they made their way to Geneva. As they approached the city, they could see the soaring spires of Saint Pierre, a welcome sight. They wound their way through the cobbled streets upward to the towering church. People of all sorts were streaming to the cathedral. The tall front doors leading into the sanctuary swung open, and they entered with the flow of worshipers. Never had they been seated in such an impressive edifice.

As the worshipers gather, their eyes are drawn to the great pulpit elevated far above the stone floor of the sanctuary. There it hangs, suspended on a massive column. Wrapping around this column is a spiral staircase that leads up to the wooden platform upon which the famed pulpit rests. John Calvin regularly stands here to expound the Word of God.

As the service begins, the Huguenots discover that only the Word of God is sung at Saint Pierre. The psalms are set to metered cadence and serve as the text for all congregational singing. The regulative principle—based on *sola Scriptura*— reigns here. As the service progresses, the assembled people sing out from the depths of their hearts. The Word preached in previous weeks and months has left its fire within them. The days of vain mantras and empty ritualism are over. Now the well-taught people raise their voices to magnify the Lord.

Following the congregational singing, the much-antici-pated time comes. Calvin rises to expound the biblical text. Hearts are astounded; souls are arrested. Under the conviction and challenge of his expository preaching, the Huguenots are galvanized in their faith. Some of them are so stirred that, amazingly, they choose to return to their native France and face the wrath of the royal guards in order to plant Protestant churches there. The preaching is *that* commanding. The truth Calvin proclaims is *that* forceful. Never before have these French Protestants heard preaching like this.

What Marked Calvin's Preaching?

Whenever Calvin assumed the pulpit at Saint Pierre, it was a momentous occasion. But what distinguished Calvin's public proclamation of Scripture? What were the hallmarks that made his preaching so successful?

Every preacher who expounds God's Word brings a body of core values with him into the pulpit. These foundational commitments inevitably shape his preaching. His pulpit ministry is governed by what he believes Scripture to be, what place he assigns to preaching, and how he believes his preaching ought to be conducted. Calvin was no exception. The fundamental beliefs that the Genevan Reformer held regarding God's Word and the centrality of the Scriptures in church life defined his preaching long before he ever stood to exposit the Word. Calvin's deeply embedded convictions about the supreme authority of the Bible *demanded* an elevated view of the pulpit. He believed the pulpit must be primary in the life of the church because Scripture is sovereign over the lives of the people. Furthermore, this commitment to the undisputed authority of the Bible compelled him to preach verse by verse through entire books in the Bible.

As we begin to consider the distinctives of Calvin's preaching, this chapter focuses on his approach to the pulpit. Before the sermon ever began, Calvin's beliefs and understandings determined the nature of his preaching.

❧ DISTINCTIVE NO. 1: BIBLICAL AUTHORITY

In Calvin's day, the primary issue of the hour was authority in the church. Church traditions, papal edicts, and the decisions of ecclesiastical councils had taken precedence over biblical truth. But Calvin stood firmly on the chief cornerstone of the Reformation—*sola Scriptura*, or "Scripture alone." He believed Scripture was the *verbum Dei*—the Word of God—and it *alone* should regulate church life, not popes, councils, or traditions. *Sola Scriptura* identified the Bible as the *sole* authority of God in His church, and Calvin wholeheartedly embraced it, insisting that the Bible was the authoritative, inspired, inerrant, and infallible Word of God.

Calvin believed that when the Bible was opened and rightly explained, the sovereignty of God was directly exerted over the congregation. As a result, he held that the minister's chief mandate was to preach the Word of God. He wrote, "Their [ministers'] whole task is limited to the ministry of God's Word; their whole wisdom to the knowledge of His Word; their whole eloquence, to its proclamation."[2] J. H. Merle D'Aubigné, the revered historian of the Reformation, notes, "In Calvin's view, everything that had not for its foundation the Word of God was futile and ephemeral boast; and the man who did not lean on Scripture ought to be deprived of his title of honor."[3] With this deep conviction about biblical authority, Calvin repeatedly entered the pulpit to minister exclusively from "the pure foundation of the Word."[4]

The Genevan Reformer knew that the authority of his preaching did not lie within himself. He said, "When we enter the pulpit, it is not so that we may bring our own dreams and fancies with us."[5] He saw the preacher—and especially himself—as merely a dispatched messenger with the divine message. He knew that "as soon as men depart, even in the smallest degree from God's Word, they cannot preach anything but falsehoods, vanities, impostures, errors, and deceits."[6] It is the expositor's task, he believed, to bring the supreme authority of the divine Word to bear directly on his listeners.

In this, Calvin admitted that he had no authority over others beyond what Scripture taught: "A rule is prescribed to all God's servants that they bring not their own inventions, but simply deliver, as from hand to hand, what they have received from God."[7] He was sure that ecclesiastical status was no license for adding to God's Word. For Calvin, any Bible teachers, small or great, who decide to "mingle their own inventions with the Word of God, or who advance anything that does not belong to it, must be rejected, how honourable soever may be their rank."[8]

This understanding of the preacher's role produced a profound sense of humility in Calvin as he rose to preach. He saw himself as standing *under* the authority of the Word. As Hughes Oliphant Old explains: "Calvin's sermons . . . [reveal] a high sense of the authority of Scripture. The preacher himself believed he was preaching the Word of God. He saw himself to be the servant of the Word."[9] T. H. L. Parker agrees: "For Calvin the message of Scripture is sovereign, sovereign over the congregation and sovereign over the preacher. His humility is shown by his submitting to this authority."[10]

Calvin's high regard for biblical authority also fueled a deep reverence for Scripture. "The majesty of Scripture," he said, "deserves that its expounders should make it apparent, that they proceed to handle it with modesty and reverence."[11] His admiration for the Bible was driven by its blend of simple teachings, profound antinomies, plain language, intricate nuances, and cohesive unity. In Calvin's view, to explore the height, depth, width, and breadth of the Bible was to revere its supernatural Author. Philip Schaff, the highly regarded Protestant historian, writes, "[Calvin] had the profoundest reverence for the Scriptures, as containing the Word of the living God and as the only infallible and sufficient rule of faith and duty."[12]

For Calvin, then, handling Scripture was a sacred responsibility. Old captures it well when he observes that "the very fact that [Calvin's] ministry was to expound the Word of God filled him with a profound reverence for the task before him."[13] As Calvin resolutely stated, "We owe to the Scripture the same reverence which we owe to God because it has proceeded from Him alone, and has nothing of man mixed with it."[14] This was the unshakable foundation of Calvin's preaching—the authority of divinely inspired Scripture. He firmly believed that when the Bible speaks, God speaks.

❧ DISTINCTIVE NO. 2: DIVINE PRESENCE

Calvin's unwavering belief in biblical inspiration led him to maintain that when the Word is preached, God Himself is actually present. He believed there is a unique manifestation of God's presence in supernatural power through the public exposition of the written Word. "Wherever the gospel is preached," Calvin declared, "it is as if God Himself came into the midst of us."[15] He added:

> It is certain that if we come to church we shall not hear only a mortal man speaking but we shall feel (even by His secret power) that God is speaking to our souls, that He is the teacher. He so touches us that the human voice enters into us and so profits us that we are refreshed and nourished by it. God calls us to Him as if He had His mouth open and we saw Him there in person.[16]

The Holy Spirit, Calvin said, is actively at work in the preaching of the Word, and this powerful ministry of the Spirit was the sine qua non of Calvin's expository ministry. He stated that during public proclamation, "when the minister executes his commission faithfully, by speaking only what God puts into his mouth, the inward power of the Holy Spirit is joined with his outward voice."[17] In fact, in all preaching, he affirmed, there must be an "inward efficacy of the Holy Spirit when He sheds forth His power upon hearers, that they may embrace a discourse by faith."[18] He believed God was not heard if His Spirit was not at work. This truth led him to say:

> Let the pastors boldly dare all things *by the Word of God*, of which they are constituted administrators. Let them constrain all the power, glory, and excellence of the world to give place to and to obey the divine majesty of this Word. Let them enjoin everyone by it, from the highest to the lowest. Let them edify the body of Christ. Let them devastate Satan's reign. Let them pasture the sheep, kill the wolves, instruct and exhort the rebellious. Let them bind and loose, thunder and lightning, if necessary, *but let them do all according to the Word of God*.[19]

On the other hand, Calvin noted that any dead orthodoxy on the preacher's part invites the judgment of God. The power of the Spirit, he said, is "extinguished as soon as the Doctors blow their flutes . . . to display their eloquence."[20] In other words, the Holy Spirit works through a preacher upon the listener only to the extent that the Word is taught correctly and clearly.

Not surprisingly, this belief in God's powerful presence in preaching had a profound influence on Calvin's view of the pulpit. He wrote, "The office of teaching is committed to pastors for no other purpose than that God alone may be heard there."[21] A life-transforming pulpit ministry, for Calvin, required the divine presence in power.

❧ DISTINCTIVE NO. 3: PULPIT PRIORITY

Further, Calvin believed that biblical preaching must occupy the chief place in the worship service. What God has to say to man is infinitely more important than what man has to say to God. If the congregation is to worship properly, if believers are to be edified, if the lost are to be converted, God's Word *must* be exposited. Nothing must crowd the Scriptures out of the chief place in the public gathering.

The primacy of biblical preaching in Calvin's thought was undeniable: "Wherever we see the Word of God purely preached and heard, and the sacraments administered according to Christ's institution, there, it is not to be doubted, a church of God exists."[22] On the other hand, "An assembly in which the preaching of heavenly doctrine is not heard does not deserve to be reckoned a church."[23] In short, Calvin held that Bible exposition should occupy the primary place in the worship service, meaning that preaching is the primary role of the minister.

But not just any sort of preaching will do. Calvin wrote, "The truth of God is maintained by the pure preaching of the gospel."[24] He added, "God will have His church trained up by the pure preaching of His own Word, not by the contrivances of men [which are wood, hay and stubble]."[25] He knew that when sound biblical preaching vanishes from the church, doctrine and piety leave with it: "Piety would soon decay if the living preaching of doctrine should cease."[26] Quite simply,

Calvin believed the church can be edified only by "the preaching of the gospel which is inwardly replete with a kind of solid majesty."[27] Biblical preaching is *that* necessary and *that* noble.

According to the Genevan Ordinances of 1542, which Calvin himself penned, the primary duty of pastors, elders, and ministers is to announce the Word of God for instruction, admonition, exhortation, and reproof,[28] and no figure in church history exemplified that statement better than Calvin himself. He declared, "The aim of a good teacher, [is] to turn away the eyes of men from the world, that they may look up to heaven."[29] Likewise, "The theologian's task is not to divert the ears with clatter, but to strengthen consciences by teaching things true, sure, and profitable."[30] *This* is true preaching.

As Reformation theology established a foothold—largely though Calvin's public exposition—dramatic changes began sweeping across Europe. Bible exposition returned to its central place in the church. James Montgomery Boice noted this realignment when he wrote:

When the Reformation swept over Europe in the sixteenth century, there was an immediate elevation of the Word of God in Protestant services. John Calvin particularly carried this out with thoroughness, ordering that the altars, long the centers of the Latin mass, be removed from the churches and that a pulpit with a Bible on it be placed at the center of the building. This was not to be on one side of the room, but at the very center, where every line of the architecture would carry the gaze of the worshiper to the Book which alone contains the way of salvation and outlines the principles upon which the church of the living God is to be governed.[31]

Calvin's convictions forced an emphasis on the priority of the pulpit. As the Bible was opened, reformation was unleashed.

✠ Distinctive No. 4: Sequential Exposition

For the duration of his ministry, Calvin's approach was to preach systematically through entire books of the Bible. Rarely was he out of a book study. "Sunday after Sunday, day after day," Parker writes, "Calvin climbed up the steps into the pulpit. There he patiently led his congregation verse by verse through book after book of the Bible."[32] Rare were the exceptions to this pattern. "Almost all Calvin's recorded sermons are connected series on books of the Bible."[33] As a faithful shepherd, he fed his congregation a steady diet of sequential expository messages.

This verse-by-verse style—*lectio continua*, the "continuous expositions"[34]—guaranteed that Calvin would preach the full counsel of God. Difficult and controversial subjects were unavoidable. Hard sayings could not be skipped. Difficult doctrines could not be overlooked. The full counsel of God could be heard.

Once the mature years of Calvin's ministry arrived, he "preached on a New Testament book on Sunday mornings and afternoons (although for a period on the Psalms in the afternoon) and on an Old Testament book on weekday mornings."[35] In this fashion, he covered major portions of the Scriptures. "The books of Scripture he is known to have preached through are: Genesis, Deuteronomy, Job, Judges, I and II Samuel, I and II Kings, the Major and Minor Prophets, the Gospels, Acts, I and II Corinthians, Galatians, Ephesians, I and II Thessalonians, I and II Timothy, Titus, and Hebrews. His last sermons were on the Book of Kings, February 2nd, and the Gospels, February 6th, 1564."[36]

A famous example of this verse-by-verse preaching is seen in his return to Geneva after his banishment three years earlier. In September 1541, Calvin reentered his Geneva pulpit and resumed his exposition *exactly* where he had stopped three years earlier—on the next verse! Similarly, Calvin became seriously ill in the first week of October 1558 and did not return to the pulpit until Monday, June 12, 1559—when he resumed at the very next verse in the book of Isaiah.[37] This man was fiercely committed to sequential expository preaching. For Calvin, "The subject to be taught is the Word of God, and the best way to teach it . . . was by steady and methodical exposition, book after book."[38]

Calvin's book studies were often protracted, lasting more than a year. For example, Calvin preached "89 sermons on Acts between 1549 and 1554, a shorter series on some of the

Pauline letters between 1554 and 1558, and 65 sermons on the Harmony of the Gospels between 1559 and 1564. During this same time, on weekday mornings he preached series of sermons on Jeremiah and Lamentations up to 1550, on the Minor Prophets and Daniel from 1550 to 1552, 174 sermons on Ezekiel from 1552 to 1554, 159 sermons on Job from 1554 to 1555, 200 sermons on Deuteronomy from 1555 to 1556, 353 sermons on Isaiah from 1556 to 1559, 123 sermons on Genesis from 1559 to 1561, a short series on Judges in 1561, 107 sermons on 1 Samuel and 87 sermons on 2 Samuel from 1561 to 1563, and a series on 1 Kings in 1563 and 1564."[39]

Whether the biblical book was long and extensive, such as Genesis or Job, or brief and short, such as the New Testament epistles, Calvin was determined to preach every verse. His preaching style was a significant contributing factor to the power of his Genevan pulpit. In effect, a growing momentum was achieved as Calvin preached consecutively through Bible books, each message building on the previous. As he unfolded the book, the power of its argument increased.

A High View of Preaching

Calvin's high view of preaching was undergirded by a high view of God, a high view of Scripture, and an accurate view of man. For Calvin, the four distinctives covered in this chapter—biblical authority, divine presence, pulpit priority, and sequential exposition—were inseparably linked. They stood or fell together.

In Calvin's words, preaching is "the living voice" of God "in His church."[40] He reasoned: "God begets and multiplies His church only by means of His Word. . . . It is by the preaching of the grace of God alone that the church is kept from perishing."[41] This was Calvin's commitment to preaching, and it must be that of all preachers based on the mandate of Scripture.

Where are such men of God today? Where are the preachers like Calvin, who will preach the Word with unwavering commitment? Where are the pastors who believe that God is uniquely with them as they mount their pulpits for the exposition of His Word? Where are the shepherds who have prioritized the preaching of the Word in public worship? Where are the expositors who will preach entire books of the Bible consecutively month after month and year after year?

A long-awaited return to *biblical* preaching is direly needed. Such was the case in sixteenth-century Geneva, and such is the case today. May God raise up a new generation of expositors who are equipped and empowered to proclaim the Word.

Notes

1. Alister E. McGrath, *Reformation Thought: An Introduction, Second Edition* (Oxford, England: Blackwell Publishing, 1993), 217. As quoted by James Montgomery Boice and Philip Graham Ryken in *The Doctrines of Grace: Rediscovering the Evangelical Gospel* (Wheaton, IL: Crossway Books, 2002), 42.
2. John Calvin, *Institutes of the Christian Religion* (1536 edition), trans. Ford Lewis Battles (Grand Rapids, MI: Eerdmans Publishing Co., 1975), 195.

3. J. H. Merle D'Aubigné, *History of the Reformation in Europe in the Time of Calvin, Vol. VII* (Harrisonburg, VA: Sprinkle Publications, 1880, 2000), 85.

4. Calvin, as quoted in J. Graham Miller, *Calvin's Wisdom: An Anthology Arranged Alphabetically by a Grateful Reader* (Carlisle, PA, and Edinburgh, Scotland: The Banner of Truth Trust, 1992), 254.

5. Calvin, as quoted in T. H. L. Parker, *Portrait of Calvin* (Philadelphia, PA: Westminster Press, 1954), 83.

6. Calvin, *Commentaries on the Book of the Prophet Jeremiah and the Lamentations, Vol. 2*, trans. John Owen (Grand Rapids, MI: Baker Books, 1979 reprint), 226–227.

7. Calvin, *Commentaries on the Book of the Prophet Jeremiah and the Lamentations, Vol. 1*, trans. John Owen (Grand Rapids, MI: Baker Books, 1979 reprint), 43.

8. Calvin, *Commentary on a Harmony of the Evangelists, Matthew, Mark, and Luke, Vol. 2*, trans. William Pringle (Grand Rapids, MI: Baker Books, 1979 reprint), 284.

9. Hughes Oliphant Old, *The Reading and Preaching of the Scriptures in the Worship of the Christian Church, Vol. 4: The Age of the Reformation* (Grand Rapids, MI, and Cambridge, England: Eerdmans Publishing Co., 2002), 131.

10. Parker, *Calvin's Preaching* (Louisville, KY: Westminster/John Knox Press, 1992), 39.

11. Calvin, *Commentary on a Harmony of the Evangelists, Matthew, Mark, and Luke, Vol. 1*, trans. William Pringle (Grand Rapids, MI: Baker Books, 1979 reprint), 227.

12. Philip Schaff, *History of the Christian Church, Vol. VIII* (Grand Rapids, MI: Eerdmans Publishing Co., 1910, 1984), 535.

13. Old, *The Reading and Preaching of the Scriptures in the Worship of the Christian Church, Vol. 4: The Age of the Reformation*, 132.

14. Calvin, as quoted in J. I. Packer, "Calvin the Theologian," in *John Calvin: A Collection of Essays*, ed. James Atkinson, et al. (Grand Rapids, MI: Eerdmans Publishing Co., 1966), 166.

15. Calvin, *Commentary on a Harmony of the Evangelists, Matthew, Mark, and Luke, Vol. 1*, 227.

16. Calvin, *Sermons on the Epistle to the Ephesians* (Carlisle, PA, and Edinburgh, Scotland: The Banner of Truth Trust, 1562, 1577, 1973, 1975, 1979, 1987, 1998), 42.

17. John Calvin, *Commentary on the Book of Psalms, Vol. 4*, trans. James Anderson (Grand Rapids, MI: Baker Books, 1979 reprint), 199.

18. Calvin, *Commentaries on the First Twenty Chapters of the Book of the Prophet Ezekiel, Vol. 1*, trans. Thomas Myers (Grand Rapids, MI: Baker Books, 1979 reprint), 61.

19. Calvin, as quoted in Pierre Marcel, *The Relevance of Preaching* (New York, NY, and Seoul, South Korea: Westminster Publishing House, 2000), 59.

20. Calvin, *Commentaries on the Epistles to Timothy, Titus, and Philemon*, trans. William Pringle (Grand Rapids, MI: Baker Books, 1979 reprint), 174.

21. Calvin, *Commentary on the Book of the Prophet Isaiah, Vol. 1*, trans. William Pringle (Grand Rapids, MI: Baker Books, 1979 reprint), 95.

22. Calvin, *Institutes of the Christian Religion, Vol. II*, trans. Ford Lewis Battles (Philadelphia, PA: Westminster Press, 1960), 1,023.

23. Calvin, *Commentary on the Book of the Prophet Isaiah, Vol. 3*, trans. William Pringle (Grand Rapids, MI: Baker Books, 1979 reprint), 213.

24. Calvin, *Commentaries on the Epistles to Timothy, Titus, and Philemon*, 91.

25. Calvin, *Commentary on the Epistles of Paul the Apostle to the Corinthians*, trans. John Pringle (Grand Rapids, MI: Baker Books, 1979 reprint), 137.

26. Calvin, *Commentaries on the Four Last Books of Moses Arranged in the Form of a Harmony*, trans. Charles William Bingham (Grand Rapids, MI: Baker Books, 1979 reprint), 230.

27. Calvin, *Commentary on the Epistles of Paul the Apostle to the Corinthians*, 176.

28. Publisher's introduction, "John Calvin and his Sermons on Ephesians," in Calvin, *Sermons on the Epistle to the Ephesians*, vii.

29. Calvin, *Commentaries on the Epistles to Timothy, Titus, and Philemon*, 283.

30. Calvin, *Institutes of the Christian Religion, Vol. I*, trans. Ford Lewis Battles (Philadelphia, PA: Westminster Press, 1960), 164.

31. Boice, *Whatever Happened to the Gospel of Grace? Rediscovering the Doctrines that Shook the World* (Wheaton, IL: Crossway Books, 2001), 188–189.

32. Parker, *Calvin's Preaching*, 1.

33. Ibid., 80.

34. Boice, foreword to Calvin, *Sermons on Psalm 119 by John Calvin* (Audubon, NJ: Old Paths Publications, 1580, 1996), viii.

35. Parker, *Calvin's Preaching*, 80.

36. Publisher's introduction in Calvin, *Sermons on the Epistle to the Ephesians,* ix.

37. Geoffrey Thomas, "The Wonderful Discovery of John Calvin's Sermons," *Banner of Truth Magazine,* January 2000, 22.

38. Publisher's introduction in Calvin, *Sermons on the Epistle to the Ephesians*, xiv.

39. Robert L. Reymond, *John Calvin: His Life and Influence* (Ross-shire, Great Britain: Christian Focus Publications, 2004), 84.

40. Calvin, *Commentaries on the Four Last Books of Moses Arranged in the Form of a Harmony*, 235.

41. Calvin, *Commentary on the Book of Psalms, Vol. 1*, trans. James Anderson (Grand Rapids, MI: Baker Books, 1979 reprint), 388–89.

CHAPTER THREE

Preparing the Preacher

Here we have the secret of Calvin's greatness and the source of his strength unveiled to us. No man ever had a profounder sense of God than he; no man ever more unreservedly surrendered himself to the Divine direction.[1]

—BENJAMIN B. WARFIELD

In all of life, one supreme passion consumed John Calvin: the glory of God. All truth revealed in Holy Scripture, Calvin believed, was intended to make known God's glory and to lead the reader to behold and adore His majesty. Likewise, sin was a frontal attack on the majesty of God; any motive, thought, or deed contrary to Scripture marred God's glory. Calvin, then, saw it as his chief duty to uphold the honor of the divine name. The cornerstone of his theology, life, and ministry was *soli Deo gloria*—"the glory of God alone."

For this reason, Calvin wrote in his last will and testament, "I have always faithfully propounded what I esteemed to be for the glory of God."[2] This was his highest aim. John Piper writes: "I think this would be a fitting banner over all of John Calvin's life and work—*zeal to illustrate the glory of God*. The essential meaning of John Calvin's life and preaching is that he recovered a passion for the absolute reality and majesty of God."[3]

Not surprisingly, this commitment to God's glory heavily influenced Calvin's biblical exegesis. When he studied, it was to behold the majesty of God. Thus, his sermon preparation was not primarily for others; it was first and foremost for his own heart. With the aid of the Spirit and a firm bent toward biblical authority, Calvin followed hard after his Creator. And as he did so, the Lord crushed his spirit and fixed within him a fearful admiration of Christ's excellencies. Week after week of careful preparation for his sequential expository preaching produced a soaring view of God that caused Calvin's mind and heart to be stayed upon his Redeemer.

Because a sermon is simply an overflow of a preacher's life, the man of God must prepare his heart well. A sermon rises no higher than a preacher's soul before God. Given Calvin's commitment to God's glory, how did he nourish his mind in the Scriptures? How did he cultivate his heart before God? What were the commitments that fueled his relentless will to be seemingly always in the pulpit? We will consider these questions in this chapter as we focus on Calvin's preparation to preach the Word of God.

❧ Distinctive No. 5: Diligent Mind

All preparation to preach begins with the mind. Calvin fully understood that he must saturate himself with the proper knowledge of the Bible if he were to magnify the divine glory. As a committed expositor, he likewise knew that a comprehensive grasp of Scripture was an absolute prerequisite for God-honoring and life-changing preaching. The pastor, he wrote, "ought to be prepared by long study for giving to the people, as out of a storehouse, a variety of instruction concerning the Word of God."[4] That is to say, the preacher can preach God's grandeur only to the extent that he understands the Bible.

This commitment caused Calvin to place a high premium on diligent study. Knowing that deep knowledge of the Bible comes only through much time in the text, he made disciplined study of Scripture a way of life, remaining in his study until the meaning was clear. He wrote:

> We must all be pupils of the Holy Scriptures, even to the end; even those, I mean, who are appointed to proclaim the Word. If we enter the pulpit, it is on this condition, that we learn while teaching others. I am not speaking here merely that others may hear me; but I too, for my part, must be a pupil of God, and the word which goes forth from my lips must profit myself; otherwise woe is me! The most accomplished in the Scripture are fools, unless they acknowledge

that they have need of God for their schoolmaster all the days of their life.[5]

Aside from his preparation to preach and lecture, Calvin's repeated grappling with specific passages of Scripture in his voluminous writings certainly deepened his knowledge of the Bible. In all, there are more than three thousand references and quotations of Scripture in the *Institutes*. His massive *Commentary on the Bible* is one of the largest Bible commentaries ever written by a single man, spanning forty-five large volumes of more than four hundred pages each. Mostly drawn from his lectures, it covers every book in the Old Testament except fifteen—three of which (Job and 1 and 2 Samuel) he preached through—and every book in the New Testament except 2 and 3 John and Revelation. Further, Calvin wrote dozens of theological treatises that were careful presentations and defenses of important biblical positions. These works covered a wide range of subjects, from church-state relations to predestination to providence to refutations of the errors of the Anabaptists and Roman Catholics.

As a result of all this study in the Word, Calvin "knew much of it virtually by memory, and most of it was available to him by quick and effective reference. Further, he had assimilated the metaphors and images of the Bible, its concepts and its nuances, into his life and thinking."[6] In short, he *knew* the Bible, having *absorbed* it in his quick memory and *embraced* it in his devoted heart. The preparation required to preach is a laborious discipline, but Calvin cut no corners.

❧ DISTINCTIVE NO. 6: DEVOTED HEART

Calvin believed not only that the mind should be filled with the truth of the Word, but that the heart must be devoted to godliness. In Calvin's view, there was no such thing as an unsanctified minister. The success of the preacher depended on the depth of his holiness. In public or private, in his study or on the street, the man of God had to be set apart from sin to holiness. Calvin remarked, "The calling of God brings [the requirement of] holiness with it."[7] For this reason, he believed that the pastor must keep a close watch over his life and doctrine. The man of God must cultivate a high view of God and tremble at His Word. Calvin wrote, "No man can rightly handle the doctrine of godliness, unless the fear of God reign . . . in him."[8]

Calvin was a truly God-fearing man, and this reverential awe *of* God purified his devotion *to* God. The rejection he experienced during his banishment from Geneva (1538–1541) served only to deepen his drive to know and serve God. When the City Council of Geneva rescinded its ban and called for Calvin's return, he wrote to William Farel, "Because I know that I am not my own master, I offer my heart as a true sacrifice to the Lord."[9] This expression of his devotion of his heart to God became the personal motto and emblem of the Genevan

Reformer. In his personal seal, the emblem is a pair of human hands holding out a heart to God. The inscription reads: *Cor meum tibi offero, Domine, prompte et sincere*—"My heart I give to thee, O Lord, promptly and sincerely." The words *promptly* and *sincerely* aptly describe how Calvin believed his life was to be lived before God, namely, in *full* devotion to Him.

In keeping with this heart commitment, Calvin continually stoked the flames of his soul through an attitude of devotion and prayer. "Two things are united," he confessed, "teaching and praying; God would have him whom He has set as a teacher in His church to be assiduous in prayer."[10] Ever and always, Calvin's preaching, teaching, pastoring, and writing—his *entire* life and ministry—were inseparably linked with fervent prayer. Through his piety, the tyranny of the many weighty matters that pressed on him lost their grip.

In Calvin's view, such piety was absolutely essential for a preacher of the Word of God. He believed that a preacher should "speak not so much with the mouth, as with the dispositions of the heart."[11] He was convinced that the man of God and his message were inseparable. He wrote, "No man is fit to be a teacher in the church save only he who . . . submits himself . . . [to] be a fellow-disciple with other men."[12] For Calvin, "Doctrine without zeal is either like a sword in the hand of a madman, or . . . else it serves for vain and wicked boasting."[13] In other words, the light of truth must yield the warmth of devotion to God. Grasping this aspect of Calvin is crucial to any right understanding of his preaching.

❧ Distinctive No. 7: Relentless Will

The zeal that marked Calvin's study and his pursuit of personal piety carried over into his work. Throughout the annals of church history, few men have thrown themselves into their preaching more fully than this Genevan. With abounding energy and unwavering focus, he proclaimed the Word of God. Simply put, Calvin was "a driven man."[14]

The Reformer's drivenness can be seen in his letter to one Monsieur de Falais in 1546: "Apart from the sermons and the lectures, there is a month gone by in which I have scarce done anything, in such wise I am almost ashamed to live thus useless."[15] It should be noted that Calvin had preached a *mere* twenty sermons that month and given *only* twelve lectures. He was hardly the idle servant he imagined himself to be.

This relentless drive in Calvin translated itself into almost-continuous exposition of the Scriptures. Every evidence is that, throughout his ministry, Calvin preached voluminously. The Genevan Reformer was seemingly *always* in the pulpit.

Little is known about his preaching schedule during the early years of his Geneva pastorate. Douglas Kelly notes, "We are not certain how often Calvin preached or precisely what books of Scripture he may have expounded during his first Genevan stay."[16] After his banishment by the City Council of Geneva, he became pastor of the French church in Strasbourg from 1538 to 1541, where he lectured or preached nearly every day, and preached twice on Sundays. Upon his return to Geneva, he seems to have preached "twice on Sundays and once on every Monday, Wednesday and Friday."[17]

In the autumn of 1542, some of Calvin's colleagues urged him to preach more frequently, and he agreed to do so. But this proved too heavy a burden, and after two months the council released him from preaching more than twice a Sunday. But he continued to preach three weekday evenings each week for seven more years:

> Prior to 1549, there were three weekday sermons at five in the evening, and three Sunday services, one at daybreak, another at nine o'clock and the last at three o'clock. After that date the number was increased to one daily sermon, and it was thereafter Calvin's constant practice, unless hindered by illness or by occasional absence, to preach at nine and three each Sunday, and, alternate weeks, to give one sermon every weekday! Thus he commonly preached no less than ten times a fortnight to the same congregation.[18]

Calvin maintained this demanding preaching schedule for the remainder of his life. So dedicated was he to the pulpit that Rodolphe Peter has estimated Calvin preached a staggering four thousand sermons in his lifetime, of which only fifteen hundred have been preserved.

Neither was Calvin a mere pulpit lecturer, detached from the lives of common saints. Rather, he faithfully shepherded his congregation on a personal level. Philip E. Hughes comments on Calvin's well-rounded efforts:

> This prolific author was also daily occupied in a multiplicity of other duties—preaching each day of every other week, lecturing three times a week in theology, always in his place at sessions of the Consistory, instructing the clergy, addressing the Council and keeping a guiding hand on the government of his city, visiting the sick, counseling the troubled, receiving the numerous callers from near and far who sought him out, and giving himself wholeheartedly to his friends in a fellowship that meant much to himself as well as to them. No wonder Wolfgang Musculus spoke of him as a bow always strung![19]

Calvin typically carried out his preaching and his other duties with little regard for his own physical well-being. His resolute will drove him to endure many ailments. For instance, he wrote to his physicians in 1564 to describe his colic, spitting of blood, ague, gout, and the "excruciating sufferings" of his hemorrhoids.[20] But worst of all seem to have been kidney stones that had to pass unrelieved by any sedative. Nevertheless, these physical setbacks scarcely slowed Calvin down. He was in the pulpit as often as health permitted, and was remarkably unwavering.

Even when Calvin was bedridden in poor health, he never

behaved like an invalid; instead, he drove himself unsparingly. His close friend Theodore Beza recalled that, in 1558, when serious illness made it imperative for Calvin to cease from preaching, lecturing, and his other pastoral and civic duties, he spent days and nights in dictating and writing letters. "He had no expression more frequently on his lips," wrote Beza, "than that life would be bitter to him if spent in indolence."[21] Eventually, Calvin did become an invalid, but he had himself carried to church on a stretcher in order to preach. Nothing would keep him from the pulpit.

If ill health never slowed Calvin, neither did opposition to his preaching. On matters to which the Bible spoke, he developed deep convictions. Through his intensive digging into the text, the truths of the Word were engraved into his soul. As a result, Calvin "believed, and so [he] spoke" (2 Cor. 4:13; cf. Ps. 116:10), even in the face of fierce persecution.

As we saw in Chapter 1, Calvin, while still a new believer, possibly wrote a speech for the rector of the University of Paris that called for reformation. He was forced to flee the city because of those views. Later, after only two years of ministry at Geneva, he was forced out of his pulpit into a three-year exile. Even when he was asked to return, the opposition was fierce. Philip Schaff writes:

> The adversaries of Calvin were, with a few exceptions, the same who had driven him away in 1538. They never cordially consented to his recall. They yielded

for a time to the pressure of public opinion and political necessity; but when he carried out the scheme
of discipline much more rigorously than they had
expected, they showed their old hostility, and took
advantage of every censurable act of the Consistory or
Council. They hated him worse than the pope. They
abhorred the very word "discipline." They resorted to
personal indignities and every device of intimidation;
they nicknamed him "Cain," and gave his name to the
dogs of the street; they insulted him on his way to the
lecture-room; they fired one night fifty shots before his
bed-chamber; they threatened him in the pulpit; they
approached the communion table to wrest the sacred
elements from his hands, but he refused to profane
the sacrament and over-awed them. On another occasion he walked into the midst of an excited crowd and
offered his breast to their daggers. As late as October
15, 1554, he wrote to an old friend: "Dogs bark at me
on all sides. Everywhere I am saluted with the name
of 'heretic,' and all the calumnies that can possibly be
invented are heaped upon me; in a word, the enemies
among my own flock attack me with greater bitterness
than my declared enemies among the papists."[22]

Calvin always persevered in ministry, never slacking before
his audience of One. Charles H. Spurgeon confessed, "I do
love that man of God; suffering all his life long, enduring not

only persecutions from without but a complication of disorders from within, and yet serving his Master with all his heart."[23]

However, Calvin was quick to credit divine grace for his endurance, affirming that "when anyone is drawn into arduous and difficult struggles he is, at the same time, especially strengthened by the Lord."[24] Calvin simply believed that strong preaching is the result of a strong drive within the preacher, and that fueled by God. He declared that mental and volitional weakness has no place in a pastor's heart. He wrote, "Nothing is more contrary to the pure and free preaching of the gospel than the straits of a faint heart."[25]

ZEAL FOR GOD'S GLORY

As a man, preacher, writer, and theologian, Calvin was unflinching in his pursuit of God. He was an ardent Bible student and an impassioned servant of the Lord. Week after week, month after month, year after year, and decade after decade, he anchored himself to the biblical text, then made it known to his people.

This tenacious study, personal piety, and relentless ministering were maintained by a passionate desire to see God glorified. For Calvin, "Teachers cannot firmly execute their office except they have the majesty of God before their eyes."[26] Even to the end, Calvin held that "The majesty of God is . . . indissolubly connected with the public preaching of His truth. . . . If His Word is not allowed to have authority, it is the same as though its despisers attempted to thrust God from heaven."[27] This focus on upholding the glory of God gave meaning to his life, his ministry, and especially his preaching.

It is desperately essential in this hour that preachers recover a soaring vision of the supremacy of God. Life-changing, history-altering preaching will come only when pastors reclaim a high view of God's blazing holiness and are overshadowed by His absolute sovereignty. Towering thoughts of God's transcendent glory *must* captivate preachers' souls.

May you be one who leaves the lowlands of trivial thoughts about God behind. A low view of God leads only to mediocrity. But a high view of God inspires holiness and a resolute spirit. May you ascend to the heights of the mountaintop and behold, as Calvin did, the breathtaking glory of God.

Notes

1. Benjamin B. Warfield, *Calvin and Calvinism* (Grand Rapids, MI: Baker Books, 1932, 2000), 24.
2. John Dillenberger, *John Calvin, Selections from His Writings* (Atlanta, GA: Scholars Press, 1975), 42.
3. John Piper, "The Divine Majesty of the Word: John Calvin, The Man and His Preaching," *Southern Baptist Journal of Theology*, 3/2 (Summer 1999), 4.
4. Calvin, as quoted in J. Graham Miller, *Calvin's Wisdom: An Anthology Arranged Alphabetically by a Grateful Reader* (Carlisle, PA, and Edinburgh, Scotland: Banner of Truth Trust, 1992), 256.
5. Calvin, as quoted in J. H. Merle D'Aubigné, *History of the Reformation in Europe in the Time of Calvin, Vol. VII* (Harrisonburg, VA: Sprinkle Publications, 1880, 2000), 84–85.
6. John H. Leith, "Calvin's Doctrine of the Proclamation of the Word and Its Significance for Today," in *John Calvin and the Church: A Prism of Reform*, ed. Timothy F. George (Louisville, KY: Westminster/John Knox Press, 1990), 223.

7. Calvin, as quoted in Miller, *Calvin's Wisdom: An Anthology Arranged Alphabetically by a Grateful Reader*, 144.

8. Ibid., 145.

9. Wulfert de Greef, *The Writings of John Calvin: An Introductory Guide*, trans. Lyle D. Bierma (Grand Rapids, MI: Baker Books, 1993), 38.

10. Calvin, as quoted in Miller, *Calvin's Wisdom: An Anthology Arranged Alphabetically by a Grateful Reader*, 251.

11. Ibid., 256.

12. Ibid.

13. Ibid., 361.

14. William J. Bouwsma, *John Calvin: A Sixteenth-Century Portrait* (New York, NY, and Oxford, England: Oxford University Press, 1988), 20.

15. T. H. L. Parker, *John Calvin, A Biography* (Philadelphia, PA: Westminster Press, 1975), 103–104.

16. Douglas Kelly, introduction to Calvin, *Sermons on 2 Samuel: Chapters 1–13*, trans. Douglas Kelly (Carlisle, PA, and Edinburgh, Scotland: The Banner of Truth Trust, 1992), ix–x.

17. Ibid.

18. Publisher's introduction, "John Calvin and His Sermons on Ephesians," in Calvin, *Sermons on the Epistle to the Ephesians* (Carlisle, PA, and Edinburgh, Scotland: The Banner of Truth Trust, 1562, 1577, 1973, 1975, 1979, 1987, 1998), vii–viii.

19. Philip E. Hughes, in *Puritan Papers, Vol. One: 1956–1959*, ed. D. Martyn Lloyd-Jones (Phillipsburg, NJ: P&R Publishing, 2000), 252.

20. Dillenberger, *John Calvin, Selections from His Writings*, 78.

21. Theodore Beza, quoted in Hughes, *Puritan Papers, Vol. One: 1956–1959*, 250

22. Philip Schaff, *History of the Christian Church, Vol. VIII* (Grand Rapids, MI: Eerdmans Publishing Co., 1910, 1984), 496.

23. Charles H. Spurgeon, *Autobiography, Vol. 2: The Full Harvest, 1860–1892*, compiled by Susannah Spurgeon and Joseph Harrald (Carlisle, PA, and Edinburgh, Scotland: The Banner of Truth Trust, 1897–1900, 1987), 29.

24. Bouwsma, *John Calvin: A Sixteenth-Century Portrait*, 259.

25. Ibid., 256.

26. Calvin, *Commentaries on the Book of the Prophet Jeremiah and the Lamentations, Vol. 1*, trans. John Owen (Grand Rapids, MI: Baker Books, 1979 reprint), 44.

27. Ibid., 254.

CHAPTER FOUR

Launching the Sermon

> *Calvin's sermons usually lasted an hour and were in the nature of continuous expositions. He began at the first verse of a Bible book and then treated it in successive sections, averaging four or five verses, until he reached the end, at which point he began another book.*[1]
>
> —JAMES MONTGOMERY BOICE

As John Calvin ascended the pulpit, an all-absorbing purpose lay before him—the faithful exposition of Scripture. His mind was not diverted by the varied tasks of the contemporary pulpit. He did not need to jump through the modern-day hoops of prolonged announcements, mostly of a trivial nature. He was not jolted by the artificial stimuli of the hard-driving music so often forced on churches today. Rather, with singularity of thought, sublimity of spirit, and spirituality of mind, Calvin stood to bring a sermon that would unveil the matchless glory of God. And it all started with a pointed and potent introduction.

Calvin's introductions allowed him to zero in on the text as soon as possible. He did not want to expend valuable time outside the passage or allow his opening remarks to distract from the main theme of the sermon. "I am naturally fond of brevity,"[2] he said, and that was especially evident in his introductions, which were direct, crisp, and to the point. Like a freeway entrance ramp, Calvin's introductions quickly brought the congregation into the flow of his thought.

Most often, Calvin began with a succinct review of the previous verses he had preached. This review was an abbreviated exposition of sorts. T. H. L. Parker noted, "After a brief preface to remind the congregation of what the previous passage had said, and thus to set the present verses within their context, he would embark on the exposition of the sentences."[3] Other times, he opted for a penetrating thought connected with the central theme of the passage.

This chapter explores the commencement of Calvin's expository sermons. How did he launch his messages? What were the goals of his opening remarks? What traits distinguished Calvin's introductions?

✵ DISTINCTIVE NO. 8: DIRECT BEGINNING

Calvin did not launch his messages with a compelling quote from another author or a pithy citation of another theologian.

He did not commence with an illustration drawn from church history or from the world at large. He did not start with an allusion to the culture or with a reference to the tumultuous times in which he lived. He did not begin with an anecdote from his own life. None of these methods are intrinsically wrong, but they were not aspects of Calvin's style.

Instead, Calvin chose to introduce his messages in a direct manner, one that immediately drew the listeners to the biblical text. Calvin was not a silver-tongued orator, but a Bible-teaching expositor. Above all else, he desired to bring his people to the Scriptures. As a result, Calvin began with a pointed statement, directing the congregation to the passage immediately before them.

Some of the beginning sentences of the sermons Calvin preached from the book of Micah are classic examples of his brief introductions. These initial lines reveal how Calvin often used his first words to orient his listeners to his text by reviewing the previous sermon's passage. It should be remembered that these sermons on Micah were preached on consecutive evenings, Monday through Saturday; this explains the repeated reference to "yesterday":

Yesterday, we saw how Micah proclaimed God's judgment against all unbelievers.[4]

In this passage, Micah demonstrates in whose name he speaks, seeing that he attributes such power and authority to His Word.[5]

Yesterday we examined what Micah says here: that because of our malice and rebellion, we are deprived of salvation, and unless God Himself should teach us, we cannot endure for long.[6]

Calvin's use of his introductions as brief reviews was especially evident in his Lord's Day preaching, when he would often deliver two sermons from the same book of the Bible, the first in the morning and the second in the afternoon from the next verses. In such sermons, his introductions served as general reviews of the previous messages. In this sense, each message built on the previous one. Such was the case, for example, with these introductions from Calvin's series on the book of Galatians:[7]

This morning, we saw that when God united us to the body of the Lord Jesus Christ, He was calling each of us to be a living sacrifice.[8]

We saw last time, that we need to have confidence in the fact that the gospel is true.[9]

This morning we made a thorough examination of the fact that although the law could not justify us or make us acceptable to God, it was not established in vain.[10]

Such brief introductions set the course for the rest of Calvin's messages. A direct beginning inevitably would launch a strong sermon.

❦ DISTINCTIVE NO. 9: EXTEMPORANEOUS DELIVERY

When Calvin stepped into his pulpit, he did not bring a manuscript of his sermon with him. But that was not because he had neglected intense study and rigorous preparation, as some have charged. In fact, the Reformer was well-prepared in the text as he stood to preach. As we have seen, he studied with utmost diligence before he approached the pulpit. As Calvin himself said:

> If I should enter the pulpit without deigning to look at a book and should frivolously think to myself, "Oh, well, when I preach, God will give me enough to say," and come here without troubling to read or think what I ought to declare, and do not carefully consider how I must apply Holy Scripture to the edification of the people, then I should be an arrogant upstart.[11]

Calvin made a conscious choice to expound the Scriptures with no preaching notes before him. Mindful that he must speak to everyday people where they lived, and not to professional theologians, he wanted his sermons to have a pastoral tone and natural delivery. Relying on the Holy Spirit, he stood before the people with only an open Bible and drew upon his thorough study of the passage. The resulting exposition was a clear, compact explanation of the text, accompanied by practical application and passionate exhortation.

Unquestionably, Calvin's brilliant mind was a key factor in his spontaneous style of delivery. Whenever he assumed the pulpit, all of his study for a particular sermon, as well as his preparation for his other teaching responsibilities, was brought to bear on the text immediately before him. In a real sense, an entire lifetime of study stood behind each message. Hughes Oliphant Old observes, "This same sort of concentration . . . enabled him to preach without notes or manuscript. . . . The sermon itself was put together before the congregation."[12]

With this extemporaneous style, Calvin sought to break from the all-too-common methodology of his day, in which the preacher merely read his sermon notes in the pulpit in a dry, lifeless manner. The Reformer said, "It appears to me that there is very little preaching of a lively kind in the Kingdom; but that the greater part deliver it by way of reading from a written discourse."[13] Thus, Calvin believed spontaneous preaching helped yield a "lively" delivery, one marked by energy and passion.

❧ DISTINCTIVE NO. 10: SCRIPTURAL CONTEXT

As his introduction unfolded, Calvin was quick to establish the context of his Scripture passage. At the outset of the message, his goal was to introduce the congregation to the thinking of the biblical author and the original recipients. More specifically, Calvin sought to show the logical reasoning of the text, why the author had proceeded from the line of thought in the preceding text to the truth he was now considering. In so doing, Calvin often showed how the particular biblical text for his sermon fitted into the building argument of the entire book.

Calvin's skill at setting forth the context of a passage is plain in these examples from his sermons on Galatians:

> Earlier, we saw that the Galatians had gone astray, despite having been faithfully taught by Paul, who had laboured diligently among them. It was not that they had completely renounced Jesus Christ, nor indeed the gospel, but rather that they had allowed themselves to be deceived so easily, and to follow false doctrines (which happens to be a very common occurrence!). They still met in the name of the Lord Jesus Christ, and practiced baptism as a sign of faith, but they had defiled their religion by adding superstition and idolatry. Thus, the Galatians still referred to themselves as part of the church of God, but had become enmeshed by many foolish teachings.[14]

> We established last time that the law came after the promise of God to be gracious to the house of Abraham. God promised free grace, and the Jews were

to lean upon this promise for their salvation, knowing that God would mercifully send them a Redeemer, through whom they would obtain remission of their sins. From this, Paul concludes that the law (which came after the promise) did not abolish that which had been ordained and established by God.[15]

As these examples show, Calvin was careful to demonstrate the greater and grander movement of the book. He understood that a text must be seen in light of the big picture in order to be properly understood. Thus, he felt he must establish the context, ever so briefly, before delving into the intricate parts of the designated passage. He first considered the forest before exploring the individual trees.

❧ DISTINCTIVE NO. 11: STATED THEME

In his introduction, Calvin also often disclosed his stated proposition for the sermon. Sometimes called the thesis statement or main claim, such a proposition announces the essence of the message in a succinct form. Because of this practice, there was rarely any doubt about what Calvin's message would address. From the beginning, the listener knew precisely what direction the sermon would take.

Calvin made such a statement in his sermon on Ephesians 1:3–4. After opening by saying, "We have already seen how St. Paul exhorts us to praise and bless God because He has blessed us," he proceeded to state his purpose in the second paragraph of the introduction:

> And now St. Paul brings us to the origin and source, or rather to the principal cause that moved God to take us into His favour. For it is not enough that God has revealed the treasures of His goodness and mercy to draw us to hope of the heavenly life by the gospel—and yet that is very much. For had not St. Paul added that which we see now, it might have been surmised that God's grace is common to all men and that He offers it and presents it to all without exception, and, consequently, that it is in every man's power to receive it according to his own free will, by which means there would be some merit in us. . . . But St. Paul, to exclude all merit on man's part and to show that all comes from God's pure goodness and grace, says that He has blessed us according to His election of us beforehand.[16]

An even more succinct theme statement appears in this example from one of Calvin's sermons on Micah:

> Now from this text, as I have reiterated, we see how opposed our Lord is to having His Word falsified; for blinding the false prophets as He does is a harsh and stiff penalty, resulting in their being disowned by God.[17]

By this practice of stating his theme in the introduction, Calvin established the framework of a building argument before expositing the text itself. In so doing, he put his listeners into the mind of the biblical author from the very outset of the sermon. Laying out the overarching argument of the book and showing how a particular passage fit into it was a significant aspect of Calvin's expository genius.

A Bridge to the Text

Calvin's preaching was supremely focused on the text of Scripture. For this reason, his introduction served as a bridge to the text—short, succinct, and straightforward. The Reformer chose not to spend prolonged time outside the text, not even in the introduction. His goal, simply stated, was to orient his listeners to the central theme of the biblical passage that lay before him. This direct approach served him well and reflected his commitment to let the Bible speak for itself.

In this present hour, we should pray to the supernatural Author of Scripture Himself, God Almighty, that all preachers would devote themselves to the exposition of the Bible. And like Calvin, may they waste no time in the pulpit, but get straight to the text. May they explicate their passages as soon as is reasonable. May their introductions serve to usher their listeners into the truth of the Word. And may such direct beginnings enhance their preaching, that God's Word should not return to Him void.

Notes

1. James Montgomery Boice, foreword to John Calvin, *Sermons on Psalm 119 by John Calvin* (Audubon, NJ: Old Paths Publications, 1580, 1996), viii.

2. Calvin, as quoted in J. Graham Miller, *Calvin's Wisdom: An Anthology Arranged Alphabetically by a Grateful Reader* (Carlisle, PA, and Edinburgh, Scotland: Banner of Truth Trust, 1992), 257.

3. T. H. L. Parker, *Calvin's Preaching* (Louisville, KY: Westminster/John Knox Press, 1992), 132–133.

4. Calvin, *Sermons on the Book of Micah*, trans. and ed. Benjamin Wirt Farley (Phillipsburg, NJ: P&R Publishing, 2003), 18.

5. Ibid., 49.

6. Ibid., 94.

7. Kathy Childress, introduction to Calvin, *John Calvin's Sermons on Galatians*, trans. Kathy Childress (Carlisle, PA, and Edinburgh, Scotland: The Banner of Truth Trust, 1563, 1997), ix.

8. Calvin, *John Calvin's Sermons on Galatians*, 204.

9. Ibid., 49.

10. Ibid., 325.

11. Calvin, in a sermon on Deuteronomy 6:13–15, as quoted in Parker, *Calvin's Preaching*, 81.

12. Hughes Oliphant Old, *The Reading and Preaching of the Scriptures in the Worship of the Christian Church, Vol. 4: The Age of the Reformation* (Grand Rapids, MI, and Cambridge, England: Eerdmans Publishing Co., 2002), 129.

13. Calvin, *Letters of John Calvin* (Carlisle, PA, and Edinburgh, Scotland: The Banner of Truth Trust, 1855–1857, 1980), 95.

14. Calvin, *John Calvin's Sermons on Galatians*, 385.

15. Ibid., 312.

16. Calvin, *Sermons on the Epistle to the Ephesians* (Carlisle, PA, and Edinburgh, Scotland: The Banner of Truth Trust, 1562, 1577, 1973, 1975, 1979, 1987, 1998), 22–23.

17. Calvin, *Sermons on the Book of Micah*, 156.

CHAPTER FIVE

Expounding
the Text

Calvin was the exegete of the Reformation and in the first rank of biblical exegetes of all time.[1]

—JOHN MURRAY

Most recent scholars have agreed that, for his time, Calvin was a distinguished textual scholar.[2]

—WILLIAM J. BOUWSMA

T he real genius of John Calvin's preaching lay in his careful handling and proper explanation of the biblical passage he was expounding. In Bible exposition, substance is to be desired above style, and doctrine before delivery. The meaning of the text *is* the text. Without the proper meaning, one does not have the text *per se*. Therefore, a false interpretation of Scripture is not Scripture.

But Calvin always *had* the text. He owned it as much as

any man has. He mined the rich veins of Scripture, digging deeply into its truth-laden quarries. In so doing, this learned theologian extracted precious gold and silver, and brought the treasured nuggets to the surface.

Calvin's astute handling of the Word makes apparent that he was an intellectual genius. But in addition to his natural abilities, he was supremely trained for his task and highly experienced. Educated in classical literature and civil law, he possessed exceptional powers of language, reasoning, logic, argument, observation, and literary analysis. Plus, the Reformer was reasonably proficient in both of the major original languages of Scripture, Hebrew and Greek. It also must be remembered that Calvin's ongoing study of Scripture had helped him accumulate a vast reservoir of Bible knowledge. In addition to his preaching, he lectured to his ministerial students three times weekly on weighty doctrinal matters, and several times revised and expanded the *Institutes*. All this work kept him immersed in the breadth and depth of Scripture. What is more, Calvin was steeped in the church fathers and their theological arguments.

Thus, as Calvin approached any text of the Bible during his Geneva pastorate, he brought with him years of intensive training, personal study, theological lecturing, and biblical preaching. He focused all his abilities and training on the scriptural text, that he might preach it properly. Church historian Philip Schaff writes: "Calvin was an exegetical genius of the first order. His commentaries are unsurpassed for originality, depth, perspicuity, soundness, and permanent value. . . . If Luther was the king of translators, Calvin was the king of commentators."[3]

This chapter examines Calvin's exegetical method. How many verses did he seek to cover in a sermon? What was his exegetical practice? What was his hermeneutic? In what ways did he convey the meaning of the passage before him? How did he connect a given biblical text with the rest of Scripture? The following distinctives reveal how Calvin handled the sacred text.

✖ DISTINCTIVE NO. 12: SPECIFIC TEXT

As the Genevan expositor stepped into the pulpit, he had before him a specific biblical text. Depending on the literary genre of that text, the number of verses he would expound varied. On the whole, he dealt with more verses from narrative passages, usually enough to cover a basic unit of the story. When preaching the prophets, he covered a smaller unit of Scripture. And when expositing an epistle, he treated a still smaller portion. The point is that Calvin always had a carefully chosen and specifically defined section of Scripture to exposit for his people.

An example of Calvin's verse distribution in preaching a narrative portion of Scripture can be seen in his exposition of 2 Samuel. Because the literary genre of this Old Testament book is narrative, Calvin covered enough verses in each sermon for the story to be unfolded and explained. His sermons covered anywhere from one verse to sixteen. Appendix A (page 134) lists the verse divisions Calvin used in preaching through the first thirteen chapters of 2 Samuel.

Another example is the layout of Calvin's preaching through the book of Micah (Appendix A), which is prophetic literature. In this expository series, Calvin preached anywhere from two to eight verses per sermon. The verse division depended on the flow of the sentences, the unit of thought, and what he desired to emphasize.

Yet another example of Calvin's sequential exposition was his preaching through the book of Ephesians. This was a noteworthy series, in part because no less than John Knox, the famous Scottish Reformer, was among Calvin's listeners. These sermons on Ephesians were at Knox's side when he died in Scotland. During this forty-eight-sermon series, Calvin preached as few as two verses, but no more than six (Appendix A), making the divisions as he felt appropriate to a proper understanding of Paul's teaching. These smaller verse divisions allowed for a meaty treatment of each particular passage.

T. H. L. Parker observes: "[Calvin's] text will vary in length from a single verse to a whole passage of perhaps ten or a dozen verses. Not infrequently he will preach two or three consecutive sermons on one verse. . . . But the general rule was for two to four verses a sermon."[4] Parker adds, "Clause by clause, verse by verse, the congregation was led through the epistle or the prophecy or the narrative."[5] As a result, Calvin's sermons are not "mealy-mouthed commonplaces or sermons which he had up his sleeves to make them serve all passages of the Scripture, like a shoe for all feet, but expositions, true, pure, plain, and proper for the text which he had to explain."[6]

❧ DISTINCTIVE NO. 13: EXEGETICAL PRECISION

Calvin insisted that the words within each specific passage were to be considered in their historical context and grammatical structure. In so doing, he sought to unfold the author-intended meaning of Scripture. Schaff notes: "Calvin is the founder of the modern grammatico-historical exegesis. He affirmed . . . the sound and fundamental hermeneutical principle that the biblical authors, like all sensible writers, wished to convey to their readers one definite thought in words which they could understand."[7]

This was the chief underlying principle of Calvin's exposition: He was always seeking to discover the "one definite thought" behind what the biblical author wrote. Calvin believed this was the expositor's first duty:

> Since it is almost his (the interpreter's) only task to unfold the mind of the writer whom he has undertaken to expound, he misses his mark, or at least strays outside his limits, by the extent to which

he leads his readers away from the meaning of his author. . . . It is . . . presumptuous and almost blasphemous to turn the meaning of Scripture around without due care, as though it were some game that we were playing. And yet many scholars have done this at one time.[8]

Schaff agrees, writing: "Calvin kept constantly in view the primary and fundamental aim of the interpreter, namely, to bring to light the true meaning of the biblical authors according to the laws of thought and speaker. He transferred himself into their mental state and environment so as to become identified with them, and let them explain what they actually did say, and not what they might or should have said."[9] This Calvin did with exceptional skill and precision.

Stressing this same point, David Puckett writes: "Calvin rarely loses sight of the fact that before one can explain how a passage applies to the person of the sixteenth century he must determine what its meaning was for the original writer's contemporaries. This means that Calvin can neither uproot a text from its immediate literary context nor neglect the environment in which the document was originally produced. The exegete may not neglect the audience to whom the writing was originally addressed."[10] He adds, "In larger textual units Calvin almost always favors the interpretation that he believes best suits the context. Any interpretation that cannot be justified contextually is, at best, improbable."[11] And

Parker concludes, "[Calvin] keeps to the historical context in the interpretation and exegesis of passages."[12]

❧ DISTINCTIVE NO. 14: LITERAL INTERPRETATION

In digging into the author's original intent in a passage, Calvin insisted on *sensus literalis*, the literal sense of the biblical text. He rejected the medieval *quadriga*, the ancient interpretation scheme that allowed for literal, moral, allegorical, and analogical meanings of a text. As an expositor, he believed he was not free to play fast and loose with a passage and impose his own meaning on it. As Calvin put it, "The true meaning of Scripture is the natural and obvious meaning."[13]

Without a literal hermeneutic, Calvin believed, all objectivity and certainty would be lost. On one occasion, he wrote, "The legitimate use of Scripture is perverted when it is enunciated in an obscure manner such as no one can understand."[14] In this vein, the Reformer stated, "The important thing is that the Scripture should be understood and explained; how it is explained is secondary."[15]

The literalism of Calvin's interpretation was directly related to the Renaissance scholars' desire to get at "the original and genuine meaning of a text."[16] In keeping with this:

Reformers, like Luther, Bucer, and Zwingli, as well as Calvin, who were all indebted to Erasmus and the humanistic method, agreed that the natural meaning of a statement was to be preferred to one arrived at by way of allegorizing or supplying a meaning other than the *literal*. . . . Allegory was contrary to the humanistic canon of interpretation; and "literalism," that is, the desire to get at an author's own mind was of its essence. So we find Calvin bent upon establishing what a given author in fact said. He criticized the church fathers, especially Augustine, Chrysostom, and Jerome, for dealing too subtly with the texts, for allegorizing and speculation. . . . He complains repeatedly that even while Augustine's remarks on a given passage are good, they are irrelevant to the purpose of its writer (on Rom. 8:28, John 1:16). Allegorizing was misunderstanding, and misunderstanding was the evil a scholar had to avoid by all means. . . . The natural interpretation of a passage for them was one that did justice to the *intention* of the author. When Calvin protested against allegorizing, he was protesting not against finding a spiritual meaning in a passage, but against finding one that was not there.[17]

In giving the literal meaning of the text, Calvin achieved his hermeneutical goal. He declared: "I have observed . . . a simple style of teaching. . . . I have felt nothing to be of more importance than a literal interpretation of the biblical text."[18] As John Leith puts it, "Calvin's purpose in preach-

ing was to render transparent the text of Scripture itself."[19]
This commitment was a key aspect of the genius of Calvin's
preaching.

❦ DISTINCTIVE NO. 15: CROSS-REFERENCES

In establishing a passage's literal meaning, Calvin often cited
other passages of Scripture. He held to the analogy of faith,
the truth that the Bible nowhere contradicts itself. The
Reformers believed that the Bible teaches one body of truth,
from Genesis to Revelation. Because it is the Word of God,
it is perfectly coherent and flawlessly consistent with itself.
Thus, they declared, *sacra Scriptura sui interpres*—Scripture is
to interpret Scripture. When seeking to determine the right
meaning of his text, Calvin was ready to appeal to other texts
of Scripture for further light and support.

However, Calvin used cross-references sparingly. It appears
that he desired not to wander unnecessarily from the primary
passage that lay open before him. Thus, his cross-references
were carefully chosen, never deviating from the central thrust
of the sermon, and always remaining within the parameters of
clear, consecutive exposition.

In Calvin's preaching, two kinds of cross-referencing are
evident. In the first, Calvin cited a passage without attempting
to quote it verbatim. The following paragraphs from his sermon
on Ephesians 4:11–12 display this type of cross-referencing:

Therefore let us not suppose that men can put themselves forward on their own initiative, for no man can know how to speak one word to the glory of Jesus Christ, except it is given him, and that the Holy Ghost govern his tongue. [1 Cor. 12:3] And in fact it is for the same reason that it is said that the holy Scripture is a wisdom which surpasses all that of man, and that the natural man understands not one whit of it, but that God has to reveal to us things which otherwise are too high and hidden from us. [Ps. 119:99; 1 Cor. 2:14] . . .

Then there was that special reason why our Lord Jesus Christ ordained the twelve apostles, [Matt. 10:1] to whom St. Paul was afterwards joined to preach among the Gentiles. [Gal. 2:7] That was like an entering into the possession of his kingdom. But after the gospel was thus authorized the office of apostleship ceased. Nevertheless they had companions and associates; they were not of equal status, but yet in commission with them, to sow the seed of salvation here and there, and St. Paul calls them evangelists. And so, writing to Timothy he said, Accomplish diligently the work of an evangelist. [2 Tim. 4:5][20]

On other occasions, Calvin directly quoted verses or passages, either by reading them, reciting them from memory, or paraphrasing them. Examples of this type of cross-referencing abound in his sermons:

> For, as Saint Paul says, "no longer is there a distinction between Greek and Jew, Gentile and Barbarian" [Colossians 3:11].[21]

> The prophet Jeremiah reproached the Jews for similar reasons. "Lo, neither pagans nor infidels desire to exchange their gods, but you, you cannot even cling to my Word!" [Jeremiah 2:11].[22]

> In Psalm 22 it says, "I am a worm, and no man; a reproach of men, and despised of the people" (Psa. 22:6).[23]

> As the Lord Jesus Christ declares, God alone is our Father (Matt. 23:9).[24]

> Well, he quotes from Moses when he said, "Cursed be he that confirmeth not all the words of this law" (Deut. 27:26). The passage had already said that whoever worships false gods is cursed (Deut. 27:15).[25]

In this use of other texts to open the meaning of the Scriptures, we see again how Calvin's vast knowledge of the Bible was used of God to edify and instruct the people of Geneva.

❦ Distinctive No. 16: Persuasive Reasoning

In explaining a text of Scripture, Calvin was always ready to argue his point persuasively. He would often contrast the truth taught in a particular passage with the absurdity of the opposite position. By showing the contrast, Calvin was able to prove the stated truth in a most convincing fashion. Such juxtaposition was his ally in affirming correct doctrine.

For instance, Calvin contrasted a works-based righteousness with an imputed righteousness that is by faith while preaching on Galatians 3:11–12. He first said:

Let us, therefore, turn away from the promise which the law gives us, for it is of no value to us, and accept the free grace of our God, who is stretching out His arms to receive us, that is, if we first rid ourselves of all pride. This is, in effect, what Paul means here. [26]

Then Calvin proceeded to show that these two systems of righteousness—works and faith—are as much polar opposites as fire and ice:

This argument discloses two opposites. Imagine this: one person claims that fire is a source of heat, and another arrives and rather obstinately argues the opposite. We might say to him, Can ice or frost create heat, then? Surely, they are opposite elements, and completely incompatible with one another! Or imagine a quarrel about whether the heat of the sun is necessary to this life of ours or not. Well, what would happen if there were no sun in the world? We would all choke on filthy air, which is only purged by the shining of the sun. Therefore, as there are opposing forces in the realm of nature, so the apostle says that we cannot be justified by both the law and the grace of God![27]

Through this contrast, Calvin showed that works and faith are diametrically opposed means for attaining God's righteousness.

In another instance, Calvin argued the foul nature of heresy, comparing it to poison:

When it comes to heresies and wicked perversions of the truth which distort everything, we should react as if we have been punched or stabbed in the stomach or neck. For in what does the life and well-being of the church consist, if not in the pure Word of God? If someone came and poisoned the meat which we needed for food, would we tolerate it? No, it would make us strike out! The same reasoning applies to the gospel. We must always raise our hands to defend the purity of its doctrine, and we must not allow it to be corrupted in any way whatever.[28]

With the help of such compelling images, Calvin employed his powers of persuasive reasoning to establish truth for his listeners.

❈ DISTINCTIVE NO. 17: REASONABLE DEDUCTIONS

Calvin also believed that reasonable inferences could be drawn from a biblical passage to help extract its meaning. Calvin did this well, as the following example from his sermons on Galatians shows:

> From this we draw the conclusion that for the Jews to abstain from eating pork or to observe various feast days, was not, in and of itself, vital to the service of God, but was intended to help people to exercise faith in Jesus Christ. Thus, the ceremonies themselves had no inherent virtue to impart; it was only that they pointed to a spiritual fulfillment. We can see clearly that God did not establish them in vain, but for the profit of His church. If we separate the ceremonies from Jesus Christ, they are of no more value than children's toys; but if we consider the one to whom they direct believers, then we will admit their great worth.[29]

At other times, Calvin's deductions came in the form of timeless principles he drew from his text. Note how Calvin did this in his sermon on 2 Samuel 6:20–23:

Let us draw from these words a good general principle: namely, in order to worship God, we do not need to look around either here or there to figure out how much we owe him. For we owe him a hundred thousand times more than we can ever pay, and though we try as much as possible, still we must confess that we are unprofitable servants (Luke 17:10).[30]

There were, of course, necessary safeguards to this reasoning process. In dealing with any biblical text, Calvin purposed not to exceed what Scripture itself taught. The Reformer was careful not to enter the realm of speculation. As Calvin said, "Where the Lord closes His holy mouth, let us also stop our minds from going any further."[31] In other words, he would say no more than Scripture.

ALWAYS EXPLAINING THE TEXT

Throughout his ministry, Calvin kept his preaching singularly focused on explaining the God-intended meaning of the biblical text. This was the heart and soul of his pulpit work. As Parker writes: "Expository preaching consists in the explanation and application of a passage of Scripture. Without explanation it is not expository; without application it is not preaching."[32] Calvin gave himself rigorously to this task. He was always explaining the text, always making known its true meaning, and always making application that rested on precise interpretation.

Only when the explanation was properly given, he believed, could the sermon move forward with life-changing effect.

This is where expositors must invest their main energies. They must commit themselves to digging into the biblical text and mining from its deep quarries the unsearchable riches of proper interpretation. This was the focus of Calvin's preaching, and it remains the sine qua non of all true exposition today. May God raise up in this hour an army of Bible expositors who are rooted in the biblical text and intent on explicating its true meaning. May they carefully explain the precise meaning of the Word to hungering saints.

Notes

1. John Murray, "Calvin as Theologian and Expositor," in *Collected Writings of John Murray, Vol. One* (Carlisle, PA, and Edinburgh, Scotland: The Banner of Truth Trust, 1976, 2001), 308.

2. William J. Bouwsma, *John Calvin: A Sixteenth Century Portrait* (New York, NY, and Oxford, England: Oxford University Press, 1988), 117.

3. Philip Schaff, *History of the Christian Church, Vol. VIII* (Grand Rapids, MI: Eerdmans Publishing Co., 1910, 1984), 524.

4. T. H. L. Parker, *Calvin's Preaching* (Louisville, KY: Westminster/John Knox Press, 1992), 84.

5. Ibid., 90.

6. Attributed to Conrad Badius, as cited in publisher's introduction, "John Calvin and His Sermons on Ephesians," in John Calvin, *Sermons on the Epistle to the Ephesians* (Carlisle, PA, and Edinburgh, Scotland: The Banner of Truth Trust, 1562, 1577, 1973, 1975, 1979, 1987, 1998), xiv.

7. Schaff, *History of the Christian Church, Vol. VIII*, 532.

8. Calvin, *The Epistle of Paul the Apostle to the Romans*, ed. David W. Torrance and Thomas F. Torrance (Grand Rapids, MI: Eerdmans Publishing Co., 1973), 1.

9. Schaff, *History of the Christian Church, Vol. VIII*, 531.

10. David L. Puckett, *John Calvin's Exegesis of the Old Testament* (Louisville, KY: Westminster/John Knox Press, 1995), 67.

11. Ibid., 64.

12. Parker, *Calvin's Preaching*, 92.

13. Calvin, *John Calvin's Sermons on Galatians*, trans. Kathy Childress (Carlisle, PA, and Edinburgh, Scotland: The Banner of Truth Trust, 1563, 1997), 136.

14. Calvin, *Commentaries on the Four Last Books of Moses Arranged in the Form of a Harmony*, trans. Charles William Bingham (Grand Rapids, MI: Baker Books, 1979 reprint), 232.

15. Calvin, as quoted in Parker, *Calvin's New Testament Commentaries* (Grand Rapids, MI: Eerdmans Publishing Co., 1971), 50.

16. General introduction in *Calvin: Commentaries*, ed. John Baillie, John T. McNeill, Henry P. Van Dusen (London, England, and Philadelphia, PA: S.C.M. Press, Ltd., and Westminster Press, 1958), 28.

17. Ibid., 28.

18. Ibid., 359.

19. John H. Leith, "Calvin's Doctrine of the Proclamation of the Word and Its Significance for Today," in *John Calvin and the Church: A Prism of Reform*, ed. Timothy F. George (Louisville, KY: Westminster/John Knox Press), 214.

20. Calvin, *Sermons on the Epistle to the Ephesians*, 363–365.

21. Calvin, *Sermons on the Book of Micah*, trans. and ed. Benjamin Wirt Farley (Phillipsburg, NJ: P&R Publishing, 2003), 224.

22. Ibid., 225.

23. Calvin, *John Calvin's Sermons on Galatians*, 508.

24. Ibid., 446.

25. Ibid., 260.

26. Ibid., 268.

27. Ibid.

28. Ibid., 154.

29. Ibid., 145–146.

30. Calvin, *Sermons on 2 Samuel: Chapters 1–13*, trans. Douglas Kelly (Carlisle, PA, and Edinburgh, Scotland: The Banner of Truth Trust, 1992), 285.

31. Calvin, as quoted in J. Graham Miller, *Calvin's Wisdom: An Anthology Arranged Alphabetically by a Grateful Reader* (Carlisle, PA, and Edinburgh, Scotland: Banner of Truth Trust, 1992), 79.

32. Parker, *Calvin's Preaching*, 79.

CHAPTER SIX

Crafting
the Delivery

Calvin did not have the warm personality of Luther.
One does not find in Calvin the oratorical elegance of
Gregory of Nazianzus nor the lively imagination of
Origen. He was hardly the dramatic public speaker
that John Chrysostom was, nor did he have the mag-
netic personality of Bernard of Clairvaux. Gregory
the Great was a natural-born leader, as was Ambrose
of Milan, but that was not a gift Calvin had. Yet,
few preachers have effected such a tremendous reform
in the lives of their congregations as did the Reformer
of Geneva.[1]

—HUGHES OLIPHANT OLD

P reaching is both a science and an art. Concerning the
science of biblical exposition, it is the God-assigned
responsibility of the expositor to dig into Scripture and extract
its one, true, literal meaning. To do this, the expositor must

work within the laws of hermeneutics to discover the meaning of words and their relationships. If he breaks these laws, no matter what else he might do right, he is not practicing true exposition.

But there is more to preaching than the science of proper interpretation. An expositor also must take up the art of preaching. Here, the issue is not *what* is said but *how* it is conveyed, not the *substance* but the *style.* There is room for diversity from one preacher to another. Exposition allows for differences of personality and temperament in the pulpit, for differences among congregations and how they may be addressed, and for differences of occasion. While there is only one correct meaning to a passage, there are multiple ways of conveying that meaning in a sermon. This difference accounts for the *art* of preaching.

John Calvin mastered both the science and the art of biblical preaching. As we saw in the last chapter, he was devoted to the pursuit of careful exegesis. His chief aim was always substance before style. But it would be wrong to assume the Genevan Reformer had no style. Although some think of him as stiff and awkward in his pulpit ministry, Calvin was well-equipped in the creative aspects of effective communication. Although he was certainly not a great orator, he was more than just a skilled exegete. Standing in the pulpit with an open Bible, Calvin skillfully painted with many bold brushstrokes of colorful human language. The resplendent hues of effective communication were on his preaching palette, ready for his use. At his disposal was an array of vivid figures of speech, rhetorical questions, biting sarcasm, compelling language, colloquial expressions, and the like. Such are the tools of the art of vivid preaching, and their effective use often separates mediocre exposition from good and even great pulpit work.

This chapter considers some of the potent colors that flowed from Calvin's tongue in his preaching. What was the Reformer's style of communication? What factors influenced his choice of words? What were his favored expressions? How did he employ questions, restatements, quotations, and transitions? Here are a few distinctives of the Reformer's picturesque communication.

❧ DISTINCTIVE NO. 18: FAMILIAR WORDS

Calvin possessed a strong command of language. The Reformer wrote his first book in Latin and preached in his native French from either a Hebrew or Greek Bible. Also, his education in classical literature enhanced his effective use of language as he preached, lectured, and wrote. But despite his remarkable learning, Calvin chose to employ simple words and understandable language in the pulpit. As a preacher, Calvin's primary aim was to communicate to the common person in the pew. He was not seeking to impress his congregation with his own brilliance, but to impact them with the awe-inspiring majesty of God. To this end, Calvin chose to preach "in the vernacular tongue, which may be . . . understood by the whole congregation."[2] Using simple language that the common people could easily grasp and digest ensured that Calvin did not speak *over* the heads of his sheep but connected *with* them.

Hughes Oliphant Old, professor at Erskine Seminary, makes this very observation about Calvin's understandable language:

> Calvin had . . . clarity of thought and expression. He knew how to use the language . . . his vocabulary was brilliant. Words are used with the greatest precision. His vocabulary is rich but never obscure or esoteric. It is never vain or contrived. . . . He often presents us with marvelous similes and metaphors such as the one . . . in his sermons on Micah, where he says the hypocrites used the Temple as armor against God's judgment and as a cape to cover their wickedness.[3]

John Broadus, a noted authority on preaching, also recognized Calvin's simple pulpit language:

> All his extemporized sermons taken down in short hand, as well as his writings, show not so much great copiousness, as true command of language, his expression being, as a rule, singularly direct, simply, and forcible.[4]

As T. H. L. Parker explains, the Reformer's vocabulary was "nearly always familiar and easy. . . . He is so intent on making himself understood that now and then he will think it necessary to explain a simple word which is nevertheless ambiguous from similarity of sound with a quite different word."[5] Parker adds:

> The word that Calvin used to describe what he regarded as the most suitable style for the preacher is "*familiere*" [familiar]. *Familiere* might be better rendered by the word "personal," used in the colloquial modern sense—to make the message of Scripture a personal matter, not just a collection of historical ideas; "so that we know that it is God who is speaking to us."[6]

Calvin also spoke in simple sentences that were easily accessible to his listeners. James Montgomery Boice writes: "There is little rhetorical flourish. His words are straightforward, the sentences simple. This is because Calvin understood his calling, as well as that of all other preachers, to make the biblical text as clear as possible to his hearers."[7] Rather than using long, prosaic sentences, as did some Puritans, the Reformer mainly used simple subject-verb-predicate sentence constructions[8] that were easy to digest. "Preachers must be like fathers," he wrote, "dividing bread into small pieces to feed their children."[9] Even the longer sentences in the English translations of his sermons were probably shorter in the original language. As he preached, Calvin's towering intellect nearly always lay "concealed, behind [his] deceptively simple explanations of his author's meaning."[10]

This simple style of communicating biblical truth was enhanced by Calvin's habit of preaching without sermon notes. That is to say, "The familiarity of speech is made possible and also heightened by his preaching extemporarily."[11] The resulting spontaneity often caused Calvin to use common clichés, colloquial expressions, verbal repetition, and, above all, simple vocabulary. This, he believed, made for easier listening, as opposed to reading from a manuscript containing polished sentences in formal language.

However, even in this free style of delivery, Calvin did use the language of the Bible. The Reformer would not give up the high ground of biblical vocabulary. "Calvin's terminology in this respect hardly moves outside the Bible," Parker observes. "Common words are 'justify,' 'elect,' 'redeem,' 'sin,' 'repentance,' 'grace,' 'prayer,' 'judgment'—in fact, all the familiar language of the Old and New Testaments."[12] Yet Calvin spoke "very deliberately,"[13] making it easy, as one observer noted, "to write down all that he says."[14] Parker notes: "Occasionally, he will explain the meaning of a word more carefully, but without ever giving the Hebrew or Greek original. . . . [Calvin] will never speak the original Greek word and will rarely refer to 'the Greek.'"[15]

As noted earlier, Calvin's sermons were unwritten and, thus, natural—a very different style of communication from his theological writings, such as his work in the *Institutes*, which underwent extensive edits and several revisions. Broadus notes this difference between Calvin's sermons and his *Institutes* and commentaries:

In these pages [of sermons] we hear Calvin, not as we do in his *Institutes*, which were so carefully written and re-worked, nor as in his Commentaries, which he also revised, but we hear him just as he spoke from the pulpit of St. [Pierre].[16]

In an unpublished letter, Calvin spoke of his simple style as an "ordinary mode of teaching."[17] Nevertheless, his close associate and fellow Reformer, Theodore Beza, commented on Calvin's locutions, noting, *Tot verba tot pondera*—"every word weighed a pound."[18]

❧ DISTINCTIVE NO. 19: VIVID EXPRESSIONS

In addition, Calvin used vivid expressions to enhance imagery in his listeners' minds. John Leith notes, "His sermons are replete with metaphors, comparisons, and proverbial images and wisdom that appeal to the imagination."[19] Most frequently, he used figures of speech drawn from Scripture itself, but many of his images had military, judicial, natural, artisan, or academic connections, and he often used common expressions drawn from routine conversations in everyday life. While humor was scarce in Calvin's pulpit, he used stimulating language and biting sarcasm that was sure to draw a smile or shock the listener—and leave a lasting impression.

As the following examples from Calvin's sermons on Galatians show, he employed vivid language to great effect:

The law prepares us for the gospel, for where men are puffed up with pride, they cannot know the grace of God. If a container is full of air, and you were to try to put liquid into it, none of it would be able to enter because the air would prevent it. We might also think of the human body. . . . If a man is starving, he will, nevertheless, have such a swollen stomach that he can take nothing in—he will be full. But he will only be full of wind and not food. The wind prevents him from taking down anything that will sustain or nourish him. The same applies to our foolish pride. We think we have everything we need, but all we have is like air which excludes the grace of God.[20]

Our forefathers had no other way of obtaining salvation than that which is preached to us today. This is a very important point, for some muddle-headed fools believe that no-one had heard the gospel in those days. Indeed, there are even some profane mockers of God who seek to limit the authority of God and of His gospel by saying that the gospel has only existed for these sixteen hundred years and that previously it was unknown. What![21]

Without a doubt, Calvin's preaching could be quite animated and dramatic. As Leith puts it, Calvin "insisted on a lively delivery."[22]

DISTINCTIVE NO. 20: PROVOCATIVE QUESTIONS

Calvin also was skilled at asking thought-provoking questions as part of his exposition. A survey of Calvin's sermons reveals his "constant use of the interrogative in which he engages his congregation."[23] Some questions were rhetorical, requiring no answer. These served to stimulate his listeners to consider the obvious point he was making—the silence of the unanswered rhetorical question would be deafening in the minds of his people. Other questions Calvin himself would answer. At still other times, the Reformer would ask a series of questions in rapid-fire succession to goad the thinking of his hearers.

Sometimes, Calvin would raise an objection by an imaginary opponent, much as the apostle Paul did in Romans 9, then issue a biblical reply. This proved to be an effective technique to arouse attention and heighten interest. For example, Calvin might say, "Now, here one could ask . . ." In so doing, he would bring controversial topics to the forefront and give explanation.

Note the skillful manner in which Calvin engaged his hearers with questions in the following examples:

> What can a dead man do? And surely we are dead (as I have declared before) until God quickens us again by means of faith and by the working of His Holy Spirit. Now if we are dead, what good can we do, or to what can we dispose ourselves?[24]

And why does he mention the fear of God's name, unless upon hearing God's Word, the very majesty of God is elicited from us? That is what happens when God confronts us. And if we reject God, or do not consider ourselves accountable to God and His Word, ought we not truly perish for such an ingratitude? What possible grounds of "ignorance" can spare us from that?[25]

In that light, do we still want Jesus Christ to be our king? . . . But we must ask, do we want God to acknowledge us as His people? Do we want Jesus Christ to declare us His own? Do we want Him to be our king?[26]

But notice! Did that make him meek? Did it make him humble himself under God's mighty hand? Did the knowledge of his sin lead him to a true repentance?[27]

❧ DISTINCTIVE NO. 21: SIMPLE RESTATEMENTS

Another means Calvin employed to explain a biblical text was to restate a verse in alternative words. He would adopt a different sentence structure and use synonyms. According to Ford Lewis Battles, Calvin was a superb explicator of Scripture because he was a master of the paraphrase.[28] He could reword Scripture with precision and clarity, "translating it into the language of the common human discourse of his own time."[29] He developed this elucidating skill through his education in liberal arts and literature, and applied it with theological and spiritual insight.

Calvin's signature formula to introduce a restatement was, "It is as if he were saying . . . ," though he might use slight variations, such as, "It's as if he were saying . . ." or, "In effect he is saying . . ." The following examples display this technique:

In sum, when Micah refers to Jerusalem here, it is as if he were saying: "Will not the green wood burn before the dry?" Which is exactly what our Lord Jesus Christ says [in Luke 23:31]. For, if ever there was a city that God wanted to spare, it was Jerusalem. Nevertheless, Micah proclaims that its downfall is coming.[30]

Thus, word-for-word, as Micah states: *Having evil in their hands, they wish to make it good* [Micah 7:3]. It's as if he were saying: "Their life reveals who they are. For their wickedness is known in their works."[31]

However, Paul is clearly referring to the bringing together of Jews and Gentiles here! In effect he is saying, "Yes, Jesus Christ was Mediator when the law was set forth, that God might humble men through Him to the end that they might receive His grace."[32]

At other times, Calvin introduced restatements by saying, "In other words . . .":

We are already liable to condemnation, even before we have heard the law; as it is written, those who have sinned without the law will nevertheless perish (Rom. 2:12). In other words, the heathen, although they have no code from which they stray, still have the inner witness of their conscience, which acts as their judge.[33]

In a final variation of this technique, he sometimes stated the verse, then restated it in the vernacular:

As it is written, "Doubtless thou art our father, though Abraham be ignorant of us, and Israel acknowledge us not" (Isa. 63:16). In other words, "though we descend from these people according to the flesh, our natural ancestry is nothing compared to our spiritual parentage which you have made possible through the person of your Son."[34]

This ability to restate a biblical text in alternative language while speaking without prepared notes was an important component of Calvin's genius as a preacher.

✄ DISTINCTIVE NO. 22: LIMITED QUOTATIONS

As Calvin expounded his passage, he supplied very few quotations from other authors. A reading of his sermons reveals limited citations from theologians or commentators. And even when Calvin did draw from other writers, he often did so in a veiled or oblique way. Calvin desired the focus to remain on the biblical writer, not extra-biblical sources. Parker writes, "The occasions when Calvin himself mentioned another author by name are rare indeed."[35]

Given the fact that Calvin preached without notes, this practice of limited citations is easily understood. The few references he made to other sources were done without the aid of the quotes written before him. Thus, his citations generally were stated in a paraphrase fashion, as in the following example:

> But, if we unhappily spurn the grace that God would offer us, then we deserve to be denied all those blessings that God has promised us, and will justly experience the misery that accompanies being separated from God.[36]

This part of Calvin's sermon on Micah 4:8–10a contains an echo of a famous statement by Augustine in his book *On Free Will*. In that classic work, Augustine wrote that souls become "miserable if they sin." Here, Calvin made a similar statement, paraphrasing Augustine—"the misery that accompanies being separated from God"—without directly citing him. No doubt, in the heat of the preaching moment, Calvin quickly drew from his sharp mind this sentence from Augustine—yet few would know it.

Calvin certainly had studied the teachings of the church

fathers. But as Leith points out, "Calvin made little use of the fathers of the church in his preaching. Likewise, he found little need for secondary aids to confirm the meaning and significance of Scripture."[37] In short, Calvin was content with "an analytical method which interprets and evaluates verse after verse, word after word."[38] He showed little concern to supplement his exposition with quotations from other authors. For Calvin, nothing must overshadow the Word.

❈ DISTINCTIVE NO. 23: UNSPOKEN OUTLINE

As Calvin preached, a clear structure of thought for the sermon existed in his orderly, brilliant mind, but no sermon outline was announced from the pulpit. As Leith puts it, Calvin "did not fashion his sermons according to logical outline."[39] That is to say, homiletical headings were not used in his expositions.

To be sure, Calvin did articulate his major thrusts, which were arranged in tight paragraphs of well-developed thought. But the arrangement of the message did not follow a stated outline with recognizable divisions. For Calvin, there were no designated points to the sermon, such as "First," "Second," and so forth. Neither were there polished, alliterative headings, such as "The *Purpose* of Prayer," "The *Particulars* of Prayer," and the like. Instead, Calvin moved through the biblical text without sharply defined major headings. There was a natural flow to the message—"sentence by sentence, sometimes even word by word, explaining what each part means"[40]—that gave it an unhindered, conversational feel.

As Calvin expounded the biblical text, he established subordinate truths that lined up under the major headings, although these supporting thrusts were not necessarily stated as such. Calvin's sermon on Job 21:13–15, the eightieth from one of his series on the book, shows this organization (see Appendix B, pages 136–139). The headings were numbered by Parker, but were not stated in the sermon.

Once again, in this practice, we see that Calvin, though he preached without notes, was hardly unprepared when he entered the pulpit. Rather, his message was organized with great detail in his brilliant mind.

❧ DISTINCTIVE NO. 24: SEAMLESS TRANSITIONS

Calvin also employed smooth transitions as he proceeded from one main thought to the next. Such transitions serve as bridges in communication, ushering the listener to the next heading of truth. Because he was concerned with the flow of thought in his messages, Calvin made sure his sermons were skillfully connected at the seams.

Consider some of the transitional phrases from his first sermon on Micah. Calvin pulled his listeners along as he introduced new paragraphs of thought with the following segues: "At the same time . . . Furthermore . . . But let us consider . . . It is time now, to summarize . . . In addition, we might wonder why . . . Now it is quite true that . . . On the contrary . . . From this example it can be seen that . . . Accordingly, we should infer from the foregoing that . . . Now from this text we glean . . . But, on the contrary, one finds . . . We now come to what the prophet adds . . . In the meanwhile, let us note . . . That, I say, is how proud and presumptuous . . . Now the prophet specifically says to them . . . That is the similarity that the prophet alludes to here . . . In truth . . . Having said that, however, we should note . . ."[41]

Transitional phrases such as these applied much polish to Calvin's profound messages. Clearly he was no sterile exegete, devoid of linguistic skills. Rather, he was a smooth, graceful, and purposeful conveyor of biblical truth.

✠ DISTINCTIVE NO. 25: FOCUSED INTENSITY

Calvin preached with riveting intensity, utterly absorbed in the biblical text as he delivered his message. This reality magnetically pulled people to him as he preached. His congregation, therefore, sat spellbound when they heard him.

Old writes, "Let us ask why Calvin was regarded so highly as a preacher. Why did people listen to him?" He then answers:

Although Calvin is never thought of as a great orator, he did have some important gifts of public speaking. He seems to have had an intensity which he focused on the text of Scripture which was so powerful that he drew his hearers into the sacred text along with him. This intensity comes from his tremendous power of concentration.[42]

Philip Schaff makes a similar observation about Calvin. The Reformer, he notes, "lacked the genial element of humor and pleasantry; he was a Christian stoic: stern, severe, unbending, yet with fires of passion and affection glowing beneath the marble surface."[43]

In Schaff's view, this internal intensity was a key aspect of Calvin's success as a pastor. He writes:

> History furnished no more striking example of a man of so little personal popularity, and yet such great influence upon the people; of such natural timidity and bashfulness combined with such strength of intellect and character, and such control over his and future generations. He was by nature and taste a retiring scholar, but Providence made him an organizer and ruler of churches.[44]

An Encouragement for All Who Preach

Far from being a bland Bible teacher, Calvin exposited Scripture in a lively, brisk style that certainly connected and resonated with his listeners. His communication was vivid, memorable, clear, smooth, and, at times, provocative or even shocking. His tone could be pastoral or prophetic. Added to this, Calvin's focused intensity drew his listeners to his words. Others may have been more eloquent, but none were more blood-earnest and captivating.

As Calvin spoke, he was always aware of "a harmony between the message and the medium by which it is expressed."[45] In other words, he believed "the medium"—that is, *how* he spoke—"must not distort the message"[46]—*what* he said. Rather, the style must support the substance. Calvin's literary style, his humanist training, his own personality, his personal intelligence, and his unique hour in history—these factors and more shaped his sermons into beautiful pieces of art, masterpieces of skilled exposition.

As preachers today give consideration to their own styles of communication, Calvin stands as a source of great encouragement. Though not as naturally gifted as some in public oration, the Genevan Reformer nevertheless was able to mark his generation and even the world through his pulpit ministry. May expositors draw strength from Calvin's example that, in the end, intangibles such as deep conviction of the truth and focused intensity in the Word will still win the day.

Notes

1. Hughes Oliphant Old, *The Reading and Preaching of the Scriptures in the Worship of the Christian Church, Vol. 4: The Age of the Reformation* (Grand Rapids, MI, and Cambridge, England: Eerdmans Publishing Co., 2002), 128–129.

2. John Calvin, as quoted in J. Graham Miller, *Calvin's Wisdom: An Anthology Arranged Alphabetically by a Grateful Reader* (Carlisle, PA, and Edinburgh, Scotland: Banner of Truth Trust, 1992), 250.

3. Old, *The Reading and Preaching of the Scriptures in the Worship of the Christian Church, Vol. 4: The Age of the Reformation*, 129.

4. John A. Broadus, *Lectures on the History of Preaching* (Birmingham, AL: Solid Ground Christian Books, 1907, 2004), 121.

5. T. H. L. Parker, *Calvin's Preaching* (Louisville, KY: Westminster/John Knox Press, 1992), 141–142.

6. Ibid., 139.

7. James Montgomery Boice, foreword to Calvin, *Sermons on Psalm 119 by John Calvin* (Aububon, NJ: Old Paths Publications, 1580, 1996), x.

8. Parker, *Calvin's Preaching*, 143.

9. Calvin, as quoted by Joel Beeke in "John Calvin, Teacher and Practitioner of Evangelism," *Reformation and Revival*, 10:4 (Fall, 2001), 69.

10. Parker, *Calvin's Preaching*, 87.

11. Ibid., 140.

12. Ibid., 141.

13. Publisher's introduction, "John Calvin and His Sermons on Ephesians," in Calvin, *Sermons on the Epistle to the Ephesians* (Carlisle, PA, and Edinburgh, Scotland: The Banner of Truth Trust, 1562, 1577, 1973, 1975, 1979, 1987, 1998), ix.

14. Ibid.

15. Parker, *Calvin's Preaching*, 86–87.

16. Broadus, *Lectures on the History of Preaching*, x.

17. Calvin, as quoted by Kathy Childress in introduction to Calvin, *John Calvin's Sermons on Galatians*, trans. Kathy Childress (Carlisle, PA, and Edinburgh, Scotland: The Banner of Truth Trust, 1563, 1997), x.

18. Theodore Beza, as quoted in Leroy Nixon, *John Calvin, Expository Preacher* (Grand Rapids, MI: Eerdmans Publishing Co., 1950), 31.

19. John H. Leith, "Calvin's Doctrine of the Word and Its Significance for Today," in *John Calvin and the Church: A Prism of Reform*, ed. Timothy F. George (Louisville, KY: Westminster/John Knox Press, 1990), 221.

20. Calvin, *John Calvin's Sermons on Galatians*, 231.

21. Ibid., 304.

22. Leith, "Calvin's Doctrine of the Proclamation of the Word and Its Significance for Today," in *John Calvin and the Church: A Prism of Reform*, 221.

23. Ibid.

24. Calvin, *Sermons on the Epistle to the Ephesians*, 163.

25. Calvin, *Sermons on the Book of Micah*, trans. and ed. Benjamin Wirt Farley (Phillipsburg, NJ: P&R Publishing, 2003), 342.

26. Ibid., 208.

27. Ibid., 403–404.

28. Ford Lewis Battles and Andre Malan Hugo, *Calvin's Commentary on Seneca's de Clementia* (Leiden, Netherlands: E. J. Brill, 1969), 79.

29. Leith, "Calvin's Doctrine of the Proclamation of the Word and Its Significance for Today," in *John Calvin and the Church: A Prism of Reform*, 212.

30. Calvin, *Sermons on the Book of Micah*, 55.

31. Ibid., 381. See Luke 6:44. This paraphrase is also a haunting echo of Philip Melanchthon's famous statement about Christ, found in his *Loci Theologici*: "Hoc est Christum cognoscere, beneficia ejus cognoscere," i.e., "Who Christ is is known in his works." For Calvin, the same may be said of a Christian.

32. Calvin, *John Calvin's Sermons on Galatians*, 321.

33. Ibid., 314.

34. Ibid., 376.

35. Parker, *Calvin's Preaching*, 88.

36. Calvin, *Sermons on the Book of Micah*, 232.

37. Leith, "Calvin's Doctrine of the Proclamation of the Word and Its Significance for Today," in *John Calvin and the Church: A Prism of Reform*, 214.

38. Ibid., 35.

39. Ibid., 217.

40. Boice, foreword to Calvin, *Sermons on Psalm 119 by John Calvin*, ix.

41. Calvin, *Sermons on the Book of Micah*, 4–16.

42. Old, *The Reading and Preaching of the Scriptures in the Worship of the Christian Church, Vol. 4: The Age of the Reformation*, 128–129.

43. Philip Schaff, *History of the Christian Church, Vol. VIII* (Grand Rapids, MI: Eerdmans Publishing Co., 1910, 1984), 258.

44. Ibid., 259.

45. Leith, "Calvin's Doctrine of the Proclamation of the Word and Its Significance for Today," in *John Calvin and the Church: A Prism of Reform*, 220–221.

46. Ibid., 221.

CHAPTER SEVEN

Applying
the Truth

There is no threshing himself into a fever of impatience or frustration, no holier-than-thou rebuking of the people, no begging them in terms of hyperbole to give some physical sign that the message has been accepted. It is simply one man, conscious of his sins, aware how little progress he makes and how hard it is to be a doer of the Word, sympathetically passing on to his people (whom he knows to have the same sort of problems as himself) what God has said to them and to him.[1]

—T. H. L. PARKER

As John Calvin stood in his Geneva pulpit, he ministered as a devoted shepherd to his beloved flock. This Reformer was a renowned theologian and peerless exegete, but he did not see those tasks as his primary role. As James Montgomery

Boice notes, "Calvin was pre-eminently a preacher, and as a preacher he saw himself primarily as a Bible teacher. . . . He saw his most important work to be preaching."[2] From his pulpit, he addressed real people who had real needs, so he spoke to them right where they lived. The goal was to bridge the gap from the text to everyday life by showing its practical relevance. Calvin rightly believed that he did not need to *make* the Bible relevant—it *was* relevant. To simply reveal its life-changing power and press it home to his listeners was his mandate.

As a preacher, Calvin was resolved to fulfill this task through every divinely prescribed means—encouragement, motivation, rebuke, reproof, correction, consolation, challenge, and so on. He knew that "merely to convey sound doctrine or correct exegesis to the mind is not preaching."[3] And he fully understood that hearing without doing was insufficient (see James 1:22). Listeners, he said, should cultivate a "willingness to obey God completely and with no reserve."[4] The Reformer added, "We have not come to the preaching merely to hear what we do not know, but to be *incited* to do our duty."[5] For this reason, Calvin believed it was incumbent upon him, as a preacher, to make careful application. He saw it his pulpit responsibility to connect the Word to those allotted to his charge.

Thus, Calvin did not fire over the heads of his people while answering the aberrations of other theologians. He did not misuse the pulpit to rebut his numerous critics. Instead, Calvin remained intent on nurturing the spiritual development of his people. He preached primarily to edify and encourage the congregation God had entrusted to him. In short, he preached for changed lives. As John Leith observes:

> Just as Calvin explicated Scripture word by word, so he applied the Scripture sentence by sentence to the life and experience of his congregation. Hence, his sermons always have a strong note of reality. They move directly from Scripture to the concrete, actual situation in Geneva.[6]

Of course, Calvin could be a polemicist when necessary. He often sounded a warning against Roman debauchery, the pope's hellish religion, and other swirling dangers of the hour. Antinomianism, semi-Pelagianism, and the fanaticism of the Anabaptists were often the objects of his rebuke. A pure gospel was his aim, to the end that unconverted souls might be regenerated. Thus, Calvin endeavored to guard the truth from all attacks. Such a defense required his constant vigil and most piercing words. But Calvin was never needlessly harsh or domineering with his own congregation, at least not intentionally. Rather, he was typically moderate in tone and gentle with his words. His objective was to build his congregation up in the things of the Lord, not tear them down. As a caring pastor, he brought the Word of God to bear on his people's lives, all for God's glory and their good.

This chapter focuses on the types of application Calvin used in the course of his sermons. How did he encourage his people in their Christian lives? What practices did he enjoin? When rebuke or confrontation was necessary, how did he undertake it? As he preached, it was Calvin's desire to connect with his listeners on many levels, and he was successful in doing so.

⚘ DISTINCTIVE NO. 26: PASTORAL EXHORTATION

Any perusal of Calvin's sermons reveals that he passionately applied Scripture with loving exhortation. In his exposition, he regularly urged his listeners to live the reality of his text. Speaking from the pulpit, the Reformer was full of warm persuasion and fervent appeal. He preached with the intent of prompting, encouraging, and stimulating his congregation to follow the Word.

Calvin often utilized first person plural pronouns—"us" and "we"—as he exhorted his congregation. By doing so, he avoiding preaching down to his listeners, but included himself in the need to act on biblical truth. In the following excerpts from his sermon on Micah 2:4–5, listen for Calvin's pastoral exhortation, urging his congregation—and himself—to practice the Word:

> Let us learn, therefore, not to become drunk on our foolish hopes. Rather, let us hope in God and in God's promises, and we will never be deceived. But if we base our hopes on our own presumptuousness, God

will strip everything away. This is one of our most essential doctrines, since human nature is so driven by presumptuousness. For we are so inflamed by an insupportable pride that God is forced to punish us harshly. We think we are so much higher than God that we ought to be more powerful than God. Consequently, seeing how inclined we are toward this vice, all the more then ought we pay heed to what Micah says here: that we must not rest content with the thought that whatever happens will happen. Rather, we must realize that so long as God's hand is upon us, we are condemned to be miserable. For there is no other cure shy of our returning to God and founding our hopes on His promises. Therein lies our surest remedy, equal to any and all disasters that might befall us.[7]

What must we do, then? Today, we do not have a specific part of the earth assigned to God's children as it was to Abraham's. But all the earth has been hallowed as a fit place for mankind to dwell. That being the case, let us walk in the fear of God, content with whatever He gives us, and, behold, we will be able to enjoy whatever part of the earth He gives us to inhabit, so much so that we will be able to say that we are God's heirs, and that we are already enjoying those benefits that He has prepared for us in heaven.[8]

As these examples show, Calvin's application was heart-searching, concrete, and strongly exhortative. When standing in the pulpit, Calvin was a master of the art of pastoral exhortation with inclusive language.

❧ DISTINCTIVE NO. 27: PERSONAL EXAMINATION

Calvin frequently called his listeners to self-examination as he applied Bible truth. Having presented the proper interpretation, he commonly urged the members of the congregation to search their hearts to see how they measured up to the passage at hand.

Calvin repeatedly challenged his listeners to engage in such self-examination as he preached through Galatians:

> We must all, therefore, examine our lives, not against one of God's precepts but against the whole law. Can any of us truly say that we are blameless?[9]

> This was not only written for the benefit of the Galatians, therefore, for we must apply it today and use it to teach all who cannot bear to hear the truth from others. If each of us were to examine himself carefully, we would find that we are all stained with sin until God cleanses us.[10]

> The way to apply this text of Paul's to our instruction is as follows: inasmuch as we are unaware of the sins

that lurk within us, it is necessary for God to come and examine our lives. . . . Yet if each of us were more careful to examine ourselves in this way, we would all surely have occasion to tremble and sigh; all haughtiness and pride would be cast down and we would be ashamed of every aspect of our lives.[11]

It was Calvin's clear desire that his people not look into the mirror of the Word, only to turn away and forget what they had seen. Instead, he called them to search their lives carefully in light of the truth he had proclaimed.

✄ DISTINCTIVE NO. 28: LOVING REBUKE

Loving admonishment often distinguished Calvin's preaching when he was aware that members of his flock were flirting with or living in sin. He openly attacked vice, knowing that his words would challenge his listeners and perhaps provoke their ire. Nevertheless, he called them to account before God and exhorted them to live holy lives.

In the following sermon excerpts, notice how Calvin directly confronted immorality and spiritual license. His attempt to preserve the integrity of the gospel in this sermon from Micah is especially noble:

Now this vice reigns today far more than it ever did in Micah's time. Indeed, much more! True, many are content to have the gospel preached, provided it does not touch them, or make them uncomfortable. But the moment one stirs a stick in their dung, or uncovers their mischief, they despise such a person. If at first, then, they applauded the gospel, once they perceive that God is about to hold them accountable for their sins, behold, they forsake it all. Thus we witness today such untold murmuring against God and God's Word.[12]

Some of the French refugees who came to Geneva brought sinful lifestyles with them. Their licentious ways were well-known. In response, Calvin called them to repentance:

Those who have come from afar should set themselves to behave in a holy manner as in the house of God. They could have stayed elsewhere to live in such debauchery; it was not necessary that they move from Catholicism to live such a dissolute life. And, in fact, there are some for whom it would have been better to have divorced themselves from the collar than to have ever set foot in this church to have behaved so badly. Some align themselves with "*gaudisseurs*" to harden them in their malice; others are gluttons and drunkards; others are undisciplined and quarrelsome. There are households where husband and wife are like cat and dog; there are some who try to "heighten" their own importance and imitate the lords without reason, and have given themselves to pomp and world superfluity. Others become so "delicate" that they don't know how to work anymore, and are no longer content with any foods. There are some gossipers and "bad mouthers" who would find something to say against the angel of paradise; and in spite of the fact they are "bursting" with vices, they want to put all their "holiness" into controlling ("blessing") their neighbors. Nevertheless, it seems to them all that God must be pleased with the fact that they made the voyage to Geneva, as if it would not have been better for them to stay on their manure than to come to commit such scandalous acts in the church of God.[13]

Calvin also addressed the promiscuous lifestyles of certain women of Geneva. The Reformer declared:

God requires of women a modesty such as that which they know their sex demands, and that there be no women who act like soldiers, such as one sees firing an *arquebuse* just as boldly as a man. . . . When one sees such things as that, [one realizes that] they are such monstrous, villainous acts, that not only are you compelled to spit upon meeting [these women], but you have to throw mud on these villains when they are so audacious as to pervert thus the order of nature.

Here, then, is the first thing God requires of a woman, and that is to have modesty, to conduct herself in all politeness, elegance ("*bonnetete*").[14]

Without a doubt, loving admonishment and reproof were a part of Calvin's preaching. This is as it should be. All true exposition of Scripture must include such correction.

❧ DISTINCTIVE NO. 29: POLEMIC CONFRONTATION

For Calvin, preaching also required an apologetic defense of the faith. Declaring that preachers must guard the truth, he wrote, "To assert the truth is only one half of the office of teaching . . . except all the fallacies of the devil be also dissipated."[15] He believed that systematic exposition necessitated confronting the Devil's lies in all their vile forms. In Calvin's view, the full weight of Scripture must be brought to bear against theological error, whether inside the organized church or outside it. This included refuting false teachers, especially the pope, who contradicted sound doctrine. At the heart of this practice was a holy compulsion to guard the glory of God, defend Christ's matchless character, and protect the purity of the gospel.

Calvin's most frequent confrontation was with the Roman Catholic Church and the pope. As the Genevan Reformer expounded the Scriptures, he was outspoken in addressing the false system by which Rome perverted the grace of God:

The Roman Catholic Church today continues the same kind of idolatrous practices that were common amongst the heathen, but in the name of the apostles and of the virgin Mary. The only things that have changed are the names of the idols! But superstition is as wicked and detestable today as it was amongst the first idolaters![16]

In the pulpit, Calvin minced no words when confronting the false teaching of the pope. Leroy Nixon notes, "If [Calvin] needed to divert himself and his hearers while getting his thought into better order, he was almost always good for a joke on or a blast against the Papacy."[17] One example is found in Calvin's sermon, "Recognizing the Supreme Authority of Jesus Christ," an exposition of Galatians 1:1–2:

The same applies to us today, for the Pope (in order to deceive this poor world of ours, and maintain his unlawful and hellish oppression) claims to be the "Vicar of Jesus Christ," in direct succession to the apostles! And then there are those vermin of clergy men under him, known as bishops—those horned beasts! (They only possess such an honourable title because deception abounds in Popery.) If we take them at their word, they have all descended directly from the apostles! Yet we must examine what affinity there is between them. If God has authorized their calling, then they ought to bear clear and infallible testimony to this fact. However, the Pope and all his followers are found guilty of falsifying and corrupting the whole teaching of the gospel. What they call the service of God is no more than an abomination in His sight. The entire system is built on lies and gross deception, for they have been bewitched by Satan himself, as most of us are already aware. But what cloak does Satan use to cover all this evil? It is the notion that there has been a continuous succession since the days of the apostles; thus these bishops represent the apostles today in the church, and whatever they say must be accepted. Well then, our task is to decide whether those who claim these things have anything in common with the apostles. If they are exercising the office of good and faithful pastors, then we will listen to them! But if they are living contrary to the pattern our Lord Jesus Christ ordained for His church, what can we say? Oh, but they claim to be in true succession to the apostles! Then let them first prove it. They pretend to have evidence of this, but it is most flimsy. We might as well add that there were just as many of these "successors" in Galatia, as there were in Rome; indeed, not only there, but in several of the places where Paul had preached—in Ephesus, Colosse, Philippi, and elsewhere! So, who are the apostolic successors now? If a man believes he has the privilege of being one of Paul's successors, he must surely go out and preach the gospel. He must produce evidence of the fact before people will accept him.[18]

Whenever he could, Calvin ran to the defense of the gospel. He was not ashamed of the gospel of God in Jesus Christ. Listen to him champion the cause of free grace:

> Let us, therefore, understand that there is no salvation whatsoever outside of Jesus Christ, for He is the beginning and the end of faith, and He is all in all. Let us continue in humility, knowing that we can only bring condemnation upon ourselves; therefore, we need to find all that pertains to salvation in the pure and free mercy of God.[19]

> Let us realize, in closing, that we cannot be Christians unless the Holy Spirit has first granted us the humility to confess that our salvation proceeds entirely from the grace of God.[20]

From his Geneva pulpit, Calvin took every opportunity to uphold sound doctrine and to refute any and all contradictions of it. He was a staunch guardian of the truth.

CALVIN'S MOST POINTED APPLICATION

There was always one man in the congregation to whom Calvin primarily directed his sermons. Whenever Calvin stood in the pulpit, he was toughest on this man. He never let this hearer off easily; he never let this man escape his evaluation. This man was present every time the Reformer preached. Indeed, he never missed a message. Still, this man was the one least impressed with the great theologian's reputation and giftedness. Who was this targeted man?

It was none other than Calvin himself. He always had himself in view in his preaching. Calvin confessed that he, the preacher, "needs to be the first to be obedient to [the Word], and that he wishes to declare that he is not only imposing a law on others but that the subjection is in common and that it is for him to make a start."[21]

This is where application must begin in every sermon—with the preacher himself. Before any expositor looks outward to the congregation, he must first look inward. One finger points out to the people, but three point back at his own heart. No preacher can take his people where he himself is not willing to go. May God give His church in this day humble and holy shepherds who practice what they preach.

Notes

1. T. H. L. Parker, *Calvin's Preaching* (Louisville, KY: Westminster/John Knox Press, 1992), 119.

2. James Montgomery Boice, foreword to John Calvin, *Sermons on Psalm 119 by John Calvin* (Audubon, NJ: Old Paths Publications, 1580, 1996), viii.

3. Publisher's introduction, "John Calvin and His Sermons on Ephesians," in John Calvin, *Sermons on the Epistle to the Ephesians* (Carlisle, PA, and Edinburgh, Scotland: The Banner of Truth Trust, 1562, 1577, 1973, 1975, 1979, 1987, 1998), xv.

4. Calvin, as quoted in Leroy Nixon, *John Calvin, Expository Preacher* (Grand Rapids, MI: Eerdmans Publishing Co., 1950), 65.

5. Calvin, *Opera quae supersunt omnia*, ed. Guilielmus Baum, Eduardus Cunitz, and Eduardus Reuss, in Corpus Reformatorum (Brunsvigae: C.A. Schwetschke et filium, 1895), 79:783. Italics in quotation added.

6. John H. Leith, "Calvin's Doctrine of the Proclamation of the Word and Its Significance for Today," in *John Calvin and the Church: A Prism of Reform*, ed. Timothy F. George (Louisville, KY: Westminster/John Knox Press, 1990), 215.

7. Calvin, *Sermons on the Book of Micah*, trans. and ed. Benjamin Wirt Farley (Phillipsburg, NJ: P&R Publishing, 2003), 84.

8. Ibid., 85.

9. Calvin, *John Calvin's Sermons on Galatians*, trans. Kathy Childress (Carlisle, PA, and Edinburgh, Scotland: The Banner of Truth Trust, 1563, 1997), 264–265.

10. Ibid., 419.

11. Ibid., 543.

12. Calvin, *Sermons on the Book of Micah*, 101.

13. Calvin, as quoted by Leith in "Calvin's Doctrine of the Proclamation of the Word and Its Significance for Today," in *John Calvin and the Church: A Prism of Reform*, 216.

14. Ibid.

15. Calvin, as quoted in J. Graham Miller, *Calvin's Wisdom: An Anthology Arranged Alphabetically by a Grateful Reader* (Carlisle, PA, and Edinburgh, Scotland: Banner of Truth Trust, 1992), 252.

16. Calvin, *John Calvin's Sermons on Galatians*, 3.

17. Nixon, *John Calvin, Expository Preacher*, 124.

18. Calvin, *John Calvin's Sermons on Galatians*, 9.

19. Ibid., 186.

20. Ibid., 233.

21. Parker, *Calvin's Preaching*, 116.

CHAPTER EIGHT

Concluding
the Exposition

John Calvin was by far the greatest of the Reformers
with respect to the talents he possessed, the influence
he exerted, and the service he rendered to the estab-
lishment and diffusion of important truth.[1]

—WILLIAM CUNNINGHAM

J ohn Calvin's expositions were full and lengthy treatments of
Scripture. He crafted them to edify beleaguered Huguenots
from France, to fortify refugees from Scotland and England,
and to evangelize Catholic souls in Geneva. He was dealing with
great and weighty issues that required meaty messages. Thus, far
from skimming over the passages he expounded, Calvin dug
deep into each text to uncover its sacred treasures. Not surprisingly, detailed explanations and cogent arguments required a
significant allotment of time to deliver. Also, the renowned
Reformer addressed his congregation with a slow cadence and

deliberate pace. Thus, Calvin's expositions were approximately one hour in length, some six thousand words each. As a faithful expositor, he invested the necessary time in the pulpit to exposit the Scriptures properly and forcefully.

But Calvin recognized that sound explication and solid application were not enough. He knew he must bring his sermons to a strong conclusion. Thus, the Reformer sought to end with a commanding climax. Last words are lasting words, and nowhere was this more true than in Calvin's pulpit. Rather than tapering off at the end, losing their force and appeal, Calvin's messages increased in momentum as they drew toward their conclusion, then ended with a direct impact that left a lasting impression on his listeners. As a symphony escalates toward a final crescendo, Calvin's expositions rose in their intensity and soared to the end, leaving his congregation lifted up to the presence of God.

In the conclusion of each sermon, Calvin first gave a short summation of the truth he had exposited. He then passionately called for his hearers' unqualified submission to the Lord. He summoned their wills to an unwavering faith in God, by which they would choose obedience from the heart. Like a skilled attorney making his closing appeal before a jury, the Genevan expositor pressed his biblical text to his congregation's souls, calling for their verdict—a decision that would honor God. Finally, he concluded with public prayer, committing his flock into the sovereign hands of the Lord. This chapter focuses on these concluding elements of Calvin's exposition.

✠ DISTINCTIVE NO. 30: SUCCINCT SUMMATION

As Calvin concluded his powerful exposition, he generally summarized and restated the main theme he had expounded with a tightly worded paragraph. This final summation served to reinforce the salient truths he had stated in the message and to seal those truths to the hearts of his listeners. The following paragraph is a representative example drawn from his sermon on Galatians 1:1–2, which focused on the supreme authority of Jesus Christ:

> Here, then, is a summary of what we must always keep in mind. Firstly, we must not measure the gospel by the reputation of those who preach it, for they will be feeble men. We are not to use this approach, otherwise our assurance of salvation will be dependent upon the merit of men, which will mean that we are resting upon this world. We are to understand, rather, that it is Jesus Christ addressing us, as it were. And how does He speak? With the authority which His Father gave Him, for He was raised from the dead by the fullness of the power of the Holy Spirit. Our Lord Jesus Christ has such authority because He was raised and exalted to heaven, and now He has dominion over every creature. Since this is so, we must submit to Him, and keep ourselves on a tight rein, as it were. We must receive His Word

and acknowledge that He is in control of our lives. We must be willing to be taught in His name; for whenever His Word is preached, though it is uttered by the lips of men, it is spoken with the authority of God. Our faith must be totally grounded upon that Word, as much as it would be if the heavens had opened a hundred thousand times and revealed the glory of God. This, I say, is the way that we are to be instructed in this world, until the day God gathers us into His eternal kingdom. This is what we are to remember whenever we are presented with the glory of the Lord Jesus Christ.[2]

Another succinct summation appears in Calvin's sermon on Micah 1:3–5a. In this case, he made it obvious for the congregation that the end of the sermon had come. In fact, he used the word *summation*:

That, in summation, is what lies behind Micah's intention. That is why he exhorts both the great and the small to submit themselves anew to God, to implore God to forgive their sins, and to acknowledge their guilt in the realization that neither group has a legitimate excuse. That, I repeat, is what we need to glean here, in order to know how to benefit from this passage.[3]

Clearly, Calvin understood the value of restating the central thrust of the sermon. No one could leave one of Calvin's sermons without knowing his main points.

❧ DISTINCTIVE NO. 31: PRESSING APPEAL

After his final summation, Calvin skillfully transitioned to a pressing appeal, one final call for a humble response. Sometimes he enjoined confession of sin and sorrowful repentance, pleading with errant sinners to cast themselves in utter dependence on God's sovereign mercy. At other times, he felt that encouragement for continued obedience was in order. Total life transformation was his objective, so he strongly challenged the wills of his people.

During these closing appeals, Calvin's style was often blunt, a methodology he attributed to the apostle Paul. He wrote:

> "It is not enough," says [St. Paul], "to preach what is good and useful. For if men were well-disposed and received what God set before them, and were so teachable that they could put their minds and hearts into line with it, to subject themselves to what is good, it would be enough to have said, 'This is what God declares to us.' But since men are malicious, are ungrateful, are perverse, ask only for lies in place of the truth, readily go astray, and after they have known God turn again

and distance themselves from Him—for this reason it is necessary," says St. Paul, "for us to be held as it were forcible, and for God, having faithfully taught us, to exhort us to persist in obedience to His Word."[4]

The preacher must speak, Calvin said, "in a way that shows he is not pretending."[5] This Calvin did—he was blood-earnest in his preaching. Listen to him exhort his congregation:

> Moreover, let us learn that God does not intend there to be churches as places for people to make merry and laugh in, as if a comedy were being acted here. But there must be majesty in His Word, by which we may be moved and affected.[6]

As he concluded, Calvin often exhorted his congregation with these words: "Let us fall before the majesty of our great God and . . ." This was a passionate call for deep humility and personal surrender to the Lord. Whatever the text, these fervent words called for the unconditional submission of all who sat under his preaching.

For example, Calvin issued the following stern challenges at the ends of two of his sermons from Galatians:

> Now let us fall before the majesty of our great God, acknowledging our faults, and praying that it may please Him to make us increasingly conscious of them,

that we might be brought to a better repentance. May we, who have been regenerated, really feel that we are being led by the Holy Spirit. If this is the testimony of our hearts, then we may boast without hypocrisy that we are in the world, but not of it. Indeed, we are pilgrims and strangers here and our eternal dwelling place is heaven—an inheritance above, which has been secured by faith, though we do not enjoy it at the present time. May it please Him to grant this grace, not to us only, but to all peoples and nations on earth.[7]

Now let us fall before the majesty of our great God, acknowledging our sins, and praying that He would make us increasingly conscious of them. May our consciences be truly pricked, that we might hate our sin and embrace His mercy, and may His grace be poured upon us in ever-increasing measure. May His hand support and sustain us in our weakness, until we are brought to holy perfection in the kingdom of heaven, which has been bought for us by our Lord Jesus Christ.[8]

As these examples show, Calvin's closing appeals were heartfelt and passionate. He simply could not step down from his pulpit without urging his listeners one last time to act on the truth he had just proclaimed. They must be *doers* of the Word, not merely hearers.

❧ DISTINCTIVE NO. 32: CLIMACTIC PRAYER

Once he had made his final appeal, Calvin concluded his sermon with prayer. Having brought God's Word to the people, he then desired to bring the people to God's throne. His intent was to leave them in the presence of the Father. These concluding prayers were vertical in their thrust, pointing his listeners upward to God. They unveiled the glorious majesty of God as Calvin made a final plea for the spiritual good of his congregation.

The following examples of Calvin's heartfelt closing prayers are drawn from his sermons on Micah:

> *Almighty God*, our heavenly Father, seeing that since antiquity it has always pleased You to extend Your grace toward Your people, as perverse and rebellious as they were; and that You have never ceased to exhort them to repentance, but have always taken them by Your hand through Your prophets; grant us also Your grace today, that Your same Word may resound in our ears; and, if at first we should not profit from Your holy teaching as we ought; nonetheless, do not reject us; but by Your Spirit subdue and so reign over our minds and affections, that being truly humbled and brought low, we give You the glory that Your majesty is due; so that being clothed by Your love and fatherly favor, we may submit ourselves totally to You, while

at the same time embracing that goodness which You have provided and offered us in our Lord Jesus; that we might never doubt again that You alone are our Father, until that day that we rejoice in Your heavenly promise, which has been acquired for us by the blood of Your only Son, our Lord Jesus Christ. Amen.[9]

Almighty God, our heavenly Father, grant us the grace that, being warned by so many examples of Your wrath and vengeance, the memory of which You have willed should endure until the end of the world, we might learn thereby how redoubtable and terrible a Judge You are against the obstinate and those who have hardened their hearts. Grant us also the grace that, today, we might not be deaf to this doctrine which we have heard from the mouth of Your prophet. Rather, grant that we might truly apply all our studies in order to appease You and find favor in Your sight, and, abandoning all hope in mankind, present ourselves directly to You. Moreover, being supported by Your lovingkindness alone, which You have promised us in Jesus Christ, may we never doubt again that You are our true Father. May we be so touched by a spirit of repentance, that, even if we have been bad examples for one another, and scandalized each other, we might rather become banner-bearers, or guides, to the right way of salvation. And may we each strive to help our neighbors by living a good and well-ordered life, so that all together we might attain that heavenly and happy life which Your only Son, our Lord Jesus Christ, has dearly acquired for us by His blood. Amen.[10]

By such prayers, Calvin made his last appeal to God on behalf of his congregation and left them *coram Deo*—before the face of God.

FROM HIM, THROUGH HIM, TO HIM

One of the great doxologies in the Bible, Romans 11:36, reads: "For from him and through him and to him are all things. To him be glory forever. Amen." In this text, which is a passionate magnification of God's sovereignty, highest glory is ascribed to Him for several reasons. First, all things are *from* Him—that is, He is the source of all that comes to pass. Second, all things are *through* Him—that is, He is the means by which all things come. Third, all things are *to* Him—that is, He is the appointed end or highest good. This theocentric realization alone gives glory to God.

This God-centeredness is uniquely true of expository preaching. Only of *biblical* preaching can it be said, truly, that all things the preacher declares are *from* Him. In this approach to preaching, the message originates in the inspired Word of God. The expositor has nothing to say apart from the Word. Further, all things the preacher says are *through*

Him. God Himself gives the expositor all that he needs for the message to come through him properly—the correct interpretation, the divine wisdom, the flaming heart, and the supernatural power to preach in a life-changing manner. Further, as the sermon is delivered, God works in the listener. He opens the eyes, ears, and hearts of those in the congregation, and He activates their wills so that the sermon might succeed. Only then can the exposition truly be *to* Him, that is, for the glory of God.

This was the passion of Calvin's preaching. Start to finish, it was *soli Deo gloria*—for the honor and majesty of God alone. From his careful study of the inspired text to the preaching itself, all things for this Genevan Reformer were *from* Him and *through* Him and *to* Him. Only of such an approach to the pulpit can it be said: *To God be glory forever. Amen.* May it be in this day that expositors in every place preach for the glory of God alone.

Notes

1. William Cunningham, *The Reformers and the Theology of the Reformation* (Carlisle, PA, and Edinburgh, Scotland: The Banner of Truth Trust, 1862, 1989), 292.

2. John Calvin, *John Calvin's Sermons on Galatians*, trans. Kathy Childress (Carlisle, PA, and Edinburgh, Scotland: The Banner of Truth Trust, 1563, 1997), 15–16.

3. Calvin, *Sermons on the Book of Micah*, trans. and ed. Benjamin Wirt Farley (Phillipsburg, NJ: P&R Publishing, 2003), 30.

4. Calvin, as quoted in T. H. L. Parker, *Calvin's Preaching* (Louisville, KY: Westminster/John Knox Press, 1992), 114–115.

5. Ibid., 115.

6. Ibid.

7. Calvin, *John Calvin's Sermons on Galatians*, 16.

8. Ibid., 33.

9. Calvin, *Sermons on the Book of Micah*, 48.

10. Ibid., 62.

"We Want Again Calvins!"

*Among all those who have been born of women,
there has not risen a greater than John Calvin; no
age before him ever produced his equal, and no age
afterwards has seen his rival.*[1]

*John Calvin propounded truth more clearly than
any other man who ever breathed, knew more of
Scripture, and explained it more clearly.*[2]

—CHARLES HADDON SPURGEON

We now stand in the twenty-first century, almost five hundred years removed from John Calvin's time, but we find ourselves in an equally critical hour of redemptive history. As the organized church was spiritually bankrupt at the outset of Calvin's day, so it is again in our time. Certainly, to judge by outward appearances, the evangelical church in this hour seems to be flourishing. Megachurches are springing up everywhere. Christian contemporary music and publishing houses seem to be booming. Men's rallies are packing large coliseums. Christian political groups are heard all the way to the White House. Yet the evangelical church is largely a whitewashed tomb. Tragically, her outward facade masks her true internal condition.

What are we to do? We must do what Calvin and the Reformers did so long ago. There are no new remedies for old problems. We must come back to old paths. We must capture the centrality and pungency of biblical preaching once again. There must be a decisive return to preaching that is Word-driven, God-exalting, Christ-centered, and Spirit-empowered. We desperately need a new generation of expositors, men cut from the same bolt of cloth as Calvin. Pastors marked by compassion, humility, and kindness must once again "preach the Word." In short, we need Calvins again to stand in pulpits and boldly proclaim the Word of God.

Charles H. Spurgeon shall have the final word here. This great man witnessed firsthand the decline of dynamic preaching and issued this plea:

> We want again Luthers, Calvins, Bunyans, Whitefields, men fit to mark eras, whose names breathe terror in our foemen's ears. We have dire need of such. Whence will they come to us? They are the gifts of Jesus Christ to the church, and will come in due time. He has power to give us back again a golden age of preachers, and

when the good old truth is once more preached by men whose lips are touched as with a live coal from off the altar, this shall be the instrument in the hand of the Spirit for bringing about a great and thorough revival of religion in the land. . . .

I do not look for any other means of converting men beyond the simple preaching of the gospel and the opening of men's ears to hear it. The moment the church of God shall despise the pulpit, God will despise her. It has been through the ministry that the Lord has always been pleased to revive and bless His churches.[3]

May Spurgeon's heartfelt prayer be answered once again in this day. We *do* want Calvins again. We *must* have Calvins again. And, by God's grace, we shall see them raised up again in this hour. May the Head of the church give us again an army of biblical expositors, men of God sold out for a new reformation. *Soli Deo Gloria.*

Notes

1. Charles H. Spurgeon, *Autobiography, Vol. 2: The Full Harvest, 1860–1892*, compiled by Susannah Spurgeon and Joseph Harrald (Carlisle, PA, and Edinburgh, Scotland: The Banner of Truth Trust, 1897–1900, 1987), 29.
2. Spurgeon, *The Metropolitan Tabernacle Pulpit, Vol. X* (Pasadena, TX: Pilgrim Publications, 1976), 310.
3. Spurgeon, *Autobiography, Vol. 1: The Early Years, 1834–1859*, compiled by Susannah Spurgeon and Joseph Harrald (Carlisle, PA, and Edinburgh, Scotland: The Banner of Truth Trust, 1897–1900, 1962), v.

APPENDIX A

John Calvin's Verse Distribution for Sermon Series

Series on 2 Samuel

1. 2 Sam. 1:1–16	29. 2 Sam. 9:1–13
2. 2 Sam. 1:17–27	30. 2 Sam. 10:1–12
3. 2 Sam. 1:21–27	31. 2 Sam. 10:10–19
4. 2 Sam. 2:1–7	32. 2 Sam. 11:1–5a
5. 2 Sam. 2:8–17	33. 2 Sam. 11:5–13
6. 2 Sam. 2:18–32	34. 2 Sam. 11:14–27
7. 2 Sam. 3:1–11	35. 2 Sam. 12:1–6
8. 2 Sam. 3:12–27	36. 2 Sam. 12:7–12
9. 2 Sam. 3:26–39	37. 2 Sam. 12:13
10. 2 Sam. 4:1–12	38. 2 Sam. 12:13–14
11. 2 Sam. 4:5–12	39. 2 Sam. 12:15–23
12. 2 Sam. 5:1–5	40. 2 Sam. 12:24–31
13. 2 Sam. 5:6–12	41. 2 Sam. 13:1–14
14. 2 Sam. 5:13–21	42. 2 Sam. 13:15–25
15. 2 Sam. 5:22–25	43. 2 Sam. 13:25–39
16. 2 Sam. 6:1–7	
17. 2 Sam. 6:6–12	
18. 2 Sam. 6:12–19	
19. 2 Sam. 6:20–23	
20. 2 Sam. 7:1–13	
21. 2 Sam. 7:4–13	
22. 2 Sam. 7:12–15	
23. 2 Sam. 7:12–17	
24. 2 Sam. 7:18–23	
25. 2 Sam. 7:22–24	
26. 2 Sam. 7:25–29	
27. 2 Sam. 8:1–12	
28. 2 Sam. 8:9–18	

Series on Micah

1. Micah 1:1–2
2. Micah 1:3–5a
3. Micah 1:5b–10
4. Micah 1:11–16
5. Micah 2:1–3
6. Micah 2:4–5
7. Micah 2:6–7
8. Micah 2:8–11
9. Micah 2:12–13
10. Micah 3:1–4
11. Micah 3:5–8
12. Micah 3:9–10
13. Micah 3:11–4:2
14. Micah 4:2–3
15. Micah 4:4–7
16. Micah 4:8–10a
17. Micah 4:10b–13
18. Micah 5:1–2
19. Micah 5:3–6
20. Micah 5:7–14
21. Micah 6:1–5
22. Micah 6:6–8
23. Micah 6:9–11
24. Micah 6:12–16
25. Micah 7:1–3
26. Micah 7:4–7
27. Micah 7:8–9
28. Micah 7:10–12

Series on Ephesians

1. Eph. 1:1–3
2. Eph. 1:3–4
3. Eph. 1:4–6
4. Eph. 1:7–10
5. Eph. 1:13–14
6. Eph. 1:15–18
7. Eph. 1:17–18
8. Eph. 1:19–23
9. Eph. 2:1–5
10. Eph. 2:3–6
11. Eph. 2:8–10
12. Eph. 2:11–13
13. Eph. 2:13–15
14. Eph. 2:16–19
15. Eph. 2:19–22
16. Eph. 3:1–6

17. Eph. 3:7–9
18. Eph. 3:9–12
19. Eph. 3:13–16
20. Eph. 3:14–19
21. Eph. 3:21–4:2
22. Eph. 4:1–5
23. Eph. 4:6–8
24. Eph. 4:7–10
25. Eph. 4:11–12
26. Eph. 4:11–14
27. Eph. 4:15–16
28. Eph. 4:17–19
29. Eph. 4:20–24
30. Eph. 4:23–26
31. Eph. 4:26–28
32. Eph. 4:29–30

33. Eph. 4:31–5:2
34. Eph. 5:3–5
35. Eph. 5:8–11
36. Eph. 5:11–14
37. Eph. 5:15–18
38. Eph. 5:18–21
39. Eph. 5:22–26
40. Eph. 5:25–27
41. Eph. 5:28–30
42. Eph. 5:31–33
43. Eph. 6:1–4
44. Eph. 6:5–9
45. Eph. 6:10–12
46. Eph. 6:11–17
47. Eph. 6:18–19
48. Eph. 6:19–24

John Calvin's Unspoken Outline of Job 21:13–15
Organized by T. H. L. Parker

1. He reminds the congregation of what he said yesterday.
2. Verse 13. "God will permit the despisers of His majesty *to go to the sepulcher in a minute of time*, after they have had a good time all their life."

   Ps. 73:4ff. (of which a brief exposition) may be compared with this passage.

   There is a contrast between the often easy deaths of the ungodly and the death-pangs of believers. But God defers His judgments to the next world; and therefore we must raise our minds above this fleeting world, when God will judge the ungodly.

   Therefore, let us not be like those who despise God and have all their happiness in this world. But rather let us prefer to be wretched here and look to God to give us His bounty hereafter.

   "See what believers are admonished of here."
3. Verse 14. "Now Job consequently declares how the wicked reject God entirely. '*They say to him, "Depart from us, for we do not wish to know thy ways."*'"

   The wicked wish to be free from God. We see them trying to get away from Him by claiming they can do as they like.

   "We do not wish for thy ways." To be near God or far from Him does not refer to His essence and majesty. It is to be obedient or disobedient to His Word.

   "Now *voici* a passage from which we can gather good and useful teaching":

   (1) The root and foundation of a good life is to have God always before us.

       (a) How can a man leave the corruption of his nature?

       (b) He must be reformed by God, for he cannot reform himself.

       (c) We are so blind that we do not know the right way.

We think evil is good until God enlightens us.

So then, do we wish to walk as we should? Let us make a start at this point—that is, of drawing near to our God. How do we draw near? First of all, let us know that nothing is hidden from Him; everyone must come to a reckoning before Him, and He must be the Judge, even of our thoughts.

"*Voilâ*, so much for the first."

(2) God will judge us by His Word, the two-edged sword.

    (a) Therefore we must draw near to Him.

    (b) And this means, to Him in His Word, in which He comes to us.

    (c) Therefore our greatest misery is to be without God's Word; our greatest blessing is when He gives it to us.

    (d) Those who will not submit to His Word show that they are God's enemies.

    (e) Let us always be willing and obedient.

    "*Voilâ*, what we have to note from this passage—that we may not only have God before our eyes, but also love Him to care for us and lead us."

4. Verse 15. "Now, after Job has shown here such blasphemy on the part of the wicked and the despisers of God, he adds that they say, *'What is the Almighty that we should serve Him and what profit will it bring us to pray to Him?'*"

    (1) The pride of the ungodly.

        (a) Pride is the principal vice of the wicked, as humility is the sovereign virtue in believers—the mother of all virtue.

        (b) Their pride is trust in their own wisdom.

        (c) Swollen with presumption, they do just what they like.

    (2) "*Who is the Almighty, that we should serve Him?*"

(a) They do not use these words, but this is in their minds; and sometimes God makes them betray themselves.

(b) They acknowledge God's existence, but not His authority.

(c) But believers must submit themselves to God as those who are His children, created in His image, redeemed by the death and passion of His only Son, and called to be His household, as children and heirs.

"When, then, we have made all these comparisons—I pray you, if we have hearts of iron or steel, ought they not to be softened? If we are swollen with arrogance and bursting with it, must not all that poison be purged, that so we may come with true humility to obey God?"

(d) He refers to the preface to the Ten Commandments: "I am the Eternal, thy God."

(i) "The Eternal"—that is, the Creator.

(ii) "thy God"—the Father of His people.

(iii) "that brought thee out of the land of Egypt, out of the house of bondage"—that is, redeemed us from the depths of hell by our Lord Jesus Christ.

(iv) Therefore we must dedicate ourselves entirely to the service of God.

(v) God adds promises to His service, that He will be our Father, the protector of our life, that He will pardon our sins, and will accept our feeble service without examining it rigorously and hypercritically.

(3) *"What is the profit of serving God?"*

(a) If we flee from God, we become servants to our own desires or to the devil.

(b) Freedom from God's service is bondage.

(c) The service of God is more honorable than possessing a kingdom.

(4) "Moreover, let us extend this even further, as Job has done."

(a) The wicked think they can live well or ill as they like, because God's punishments are not apparent.

(b) But we must hold to the truth of what Isaiah said: "There is good fruit for the righteous" (3:10). When we see confusion in the world and it seems a mockery to serve God, we must trust in Him that He will not disappoint our hope.

(c) God Himself is our reward, as it says in Ps. 16:5 and Gen. 15:1.

5. "Now, there is still one word to note. It is that after Job had spoken of the service of God, in the second place he put prayer."

(1) Although service to our fellows is service to God, more is required—"prayers and orisons."

(2) A life unstained by gross vices and yet without religion or faith is not acceptable to God.

(3) The principal service of God is to call upon Him.

(4) The conclusion: A life approved and accepted by God is one that trusts in Him and has recourse to Him and is loving toward our neighbors. "When, then, our life is thus ruled, it is the true service of God."

Bidding to prayer, relevant to the substance of the sermon.

About the Author

D r. Steven J. Lawson is the senior pastor of Christ Fellowship Baptist Church in Mobile, Alabama, having served as a pastor in Arkansas and Alabama for twenty-five years. He is a graduate of Texas Tech University (B.B.A.), Dallas Theological Seminary (Th.M.), and Reformed Theological Seminary (D.Min.).

Dr. Lawson is the author of thirteen books, his most recent being *Foundations of Grace* and *Psalms, Volume II* (Psalms 76–150) in the Holman Old Testament Commentary Series. His other books include *Famine in the Land: A Passionate Call to Expository Preaching; Psalms, Volume I* (Psalms 1–75) and *Job* in the Holman Old Testament Commentary Series; *Made in Our Image; Absolutely Sure; The Legacy;* and *Faith Under Fire*. His books have been translated into various languages around the world, including Russian, Italian, Portuguese, Spanish, and the Indonesian language.

He has contributed several articles to *Bibliotheca Sacra, The Southern Baptist Journal of Theology, Faith and Mission, Decision* magazine, and *Discipleship Journal*, among other journals and magazines.

Dr. Lawson's pulpit ministry takes him around the world,

most recently to Russia, Ukraine, Wales, England, Ireland, Germany, and many conferences in the United States, including The Shepherd's Conference and Resolved at Grace Community Church in Sun Valley, California.

He is president of New Reformation, a ministry designed to bring about biblical reformation in the church today. He serves on the executive board of The Master's Seminary and College, teaches expository preaching at The Master's Seminary in the doctor of ministry program, and teaches in The Expositor's Institute at Grace Community Church. Dr. Lawson has participated in the Distinguished Scholars Lecture Series at The Master's Seminary, lecturing in 2004 on "Expository Preaching of the Psalms." He also serves on the advisory council for Samara Preachers' Institute and Theological Seminary in Samara, Russia.

Dr. Lawson and his wife, Anne, have three sons, Andrew, James, and John, and a daughter, Grace Anne.

The "Long Line of Godly Men" Series

From the lawgiver Moses to the apostle John, and from the early church fathers to modern defenders of the faith, there has marched onto the stage of human history a long line of godly men, a triumphant parade of spiritual stalwarts who have upheld the doctrines of grace. In this five-volume series from Reformation Trust Publishing, Dr. Steven J. Lawson surveys this line of men and the biblical truth they proclaimed.

Volume One: *Foundations of Grace* 1400 BC – AD 100	Now available
Volume Two: *Pillars of Grace* 1st – 14th centuries	Coming soon
Volume Three: *Forces of Grace* 15th – 17th centuries	Coming soon
Volume Four: *Progress of Grace* 17th – 19th centuries	Coming soon
Volume Five: *Triumph of Grace* 19th century – the present	Coming soon

The "Long Line" Profiles

The men of the "Long Line" were especially gifted by God to serve His church in many ways. These books will focus in on the ways in which these men discovered, honed, and employed their gifts, affording insights for God's servants today.

The Expository Genius of John Calvin, by Dr. Steven J. Lawson

Look for future "Long Line" Profiles on Martin Luther, George Whitefield, Jonathan Edwards, Charles Spurgeon, and others.